From the Library

Family Under Fire

Family
Under Fire

A Conference Book

by

Dr. James Dobson

Beacon Hill Press of Kansas City
Kansas City, Missouri

ISBN: 0-8341-0452-0

Printed in the
United States of America

Index of Topics

How This Book Came into Being

Family Under Fire, as the title implies, is a book which was motivated by my intense personal concern for the future of the family. We have all witnessed the devastating cultural and attitudinal changes which have rocked the foundation of marriage and parenthood during the past decade. Divorce, unwed motherhood, alcoholism, suicide, cohabitation, sexual perversion, and child abuse are now everyday occurrences. I dealt last week, for example, with an eight-year-old girl who has been sexually assaulted by her alcoholic father since she was 15 months of age. How my heart groans for this vulnerable little child who has been twisted and warped by the awful circumstances into which she was born. But it is not just exceptionally pathological homes which concern me. Even loving Christian families often find themselves struggling for survival in an atmosphere of anxiety and stress. As David wrote in the Psalms, "If the foundations be destroyed, what can the righteous do?"

There are many professionals today who believe the family unit is passe and should be abandoned. Dr. David Cooper first voiced that revolutionary view in his book *Death of the Family.* Now his opinions are shared widely within professional circles. *Time* magazine expressed a similar lack of confidence in the family on April 12, 1976:

> From the founding of the nation and well into the 20th century, the family was seen as the keystone to both personal and social well-being. Writes Sociologist Sheila M. Rothman of the Center for Policy Research in New York: "The fundamental assumption was that the good order of society depended finally on the good order of the family, its ability to instill discipline and regularity in its members. Success in this mission augured well for the safety of the republic. Failure jeopardized the experiment that was democracy."
>
> But that view has changed. What Rothman calls the "discovery of personhood" leads often to the notion that happiness rests not with the family unit, but perhaps in opposition to it. The rapidly changing sense of women's proper roles, the uncertainty over children's rights, doubts about the very worth of having and rearing children, the ever-loosening legal bonds of marriage—all these have brought into question, in Rothman's phrase, "the legitimacy of the family."

I couldn't disagree more strongly with those who want to destroy the traditional family relationships. The institutions of marriage and parenthood were not the inventions of mere men and women; they were designed and sanctioned by God Almighty. *He* created the family and the principles which make it work. And if we deviate from His plan to substitute on our puny schemes, we will witness (I believe) the disintegration of everything of value and meaning. Our homes, our government, our institutions, our way of life, our society . . . *everything* rests on the stability of the family unit, and to tamper with the ground floor is to threaten the entire superstructure!

What are we to do, then, to preserve the relationships which are so fundamental and essential? I think it is high time that we mobilize our resources . . . both inside and outside the Christian Church . . . for the resuscitation of the family. It was this specific need that led to the manuscript which you are about to read. Six representatives from various professions were invited to our home in Arcadia, Calif., to discuss the nature of the problem and to suggest ways we can help. Many of our comments were addressed to the Christian Church, for it can have a powerful impact if its energies can be aroused and focused.

Sitting in my living room, then, were the following individuals who were convened from around the United States:

Dr. Paul Cunningham is pastor of the College Church of the Nazarene in Olathe, Kans. His congregation numbers approximately 1,400 each Sunday, and he shares our concern for the many families he represents.

Dr. David Hernandez is an obstetrician and gynecologist at the University of Southern California School of Medicine, and at Loma Linda University. He also maintains a private practice in Los Angeles.

Rev. James Dobson, Sr., my own father, has been a minister in the Church of the Nazarene for 42 years, and is now serving as a professor at Mid-America Nazarene College. His influence on my values and attitudes has been profound, even to the present time.

Mrs. Aarlie Hull is a housewife and mother of three children, and is married to an orthopedic surgeon. She writes a regular column for the *Herald of Holiness* and other publications, and lives in Centralia, Wash.

Mr. Jim Davis is a teacher and coach for junior and high school students in Bend, Ore. He is a "natural" leader of teen-agers and is a deeply committed layman in his home church.

Dr. Neil Wiseman is a professor and chaplain at Trevecca Nazarene College in Nashville, Tenn., and was commissioned by the Church of the Nazarene to work with me in the preparation of this manuscript.

This team joined with me for two exciting and stimulating days in the company of a court reporter who captured our conversations. There were times of intense emotion, particularly toward the end of the second day, when the Spirit of God was very evident in our midst. We feel that our effort was guided by Him, and we each dedicate this book to His purposes.

With that introduction, then, the actual discussion follows.

—JAMES DOBSON, PH.D.

The Feminine Role

Dr. Dobson, Jr.: Our purpose during the next two days will be to examine the issues which threaten the stability of family life, and offer some specific suggestions to church leaders and individual family members. There are dozens of vitally important topics which relate to this theme, but perhaps we should begin by discussing the traditional roles of men and women in our society. The feminine role, particularly, is in a state of upheaval today. Many women seem to be questioning the values and attitudes that they were taught from early childhood, resulting in an "identity crisis" of serious proportions.

With that brief introduction, then, let's plunge into these family issues with an openness and an honest desire to be used by God.

Mrs. Hull: Jim [Dobson, Jr.], you stated in your book *What Wives Wish . . .** that mothers should not work outside their homes unless it was necessary. I'd like to

---

**What Wives Wish Their Husbands Knew About Women,* James Dobson, Ph.D., published by Tyndale House Publishers, Wheaton, Ill., 1975.

know what kind of reaction you've had to that viewpoint from your readers.

Dr. Dobson, Jr.: I've received only about five letters on that particular issue, although more than 100,000 copies of the book have been sold and hundreds of other letters have been received. Nevertheless, I recognize that what I wrote is controversial and somewhat unpopular today.

Mr. Davis: I think it would be helpful if you would express your opinions here.

Dr. Dobson, Jr.: My primary concern is in regard to the welfare of the *preschool* child. Those first five years are so dynamic and critically important to later life, because the foundations are laid during that time. A child's future attitudes and values, his love for God, and his self-concept are rooted in the early years. That's why I'm concerned by the trend toward young mothers working and fathers carrying two or three simulataneous jobs. There is no baby-sitter or child care center that can take the place of a pair of concerned parents. No one else will make the investment that a toddler requires. I realize I stand pretty much alone on this matter, but that neither makes me right nor wrong.

Mrs. Hull: Dave, how do you feel about "working mothers"?

Dr. Hernandez: I agree with Jim. I feel very strongly that mothers should stay at home during the early developmental years of their children. I guess I feel so adamantly because in my medical practice, I've seen many homes devastated by mothers and fathers who thought only of their careers.

Dr. Wiseman: I don't hear you making any room for the woman who can be a good mother and a career woman at the same time. I think there are some women who can do both . . . the same way that you can be a doctor at Children's Hospital and have your time-consuming vocations and still be a decent husband and father. My wife works and finds fulfillment in her job, but she's also a very good homemaker. However, she did stay home most of the time when our kids were small.

Dr. Dobson, Jr.: There are two things that make the difference. First, your children are older. I'm not sure that my wife will want to stay home when our children are teen-agers, although that remains to be seen. The point is that *young* children are the ones who need "mothering." Second, most women are not blessed with the abundant energy necessary to handle both employment and home responsibilities. I simply haven't seen very many mothers who had the physical resources to get up early in the morning, feed and clothe their families, haul the babies to a child care center, then go to work for eight or nine hours, pick up the kids, go by the grocery store, hurry to fix dinner, clean up the mess, give the kids their baths, and then try to meet their emotional and intellectual and moral needs in the closing moments of the day (to say nothing about the sexual and emotional needs of their husbands). Not only must a loving mother do all of this one time, but she'll also face it tomorrow and tomorrow and tomorrow. For most women, *it can't be done!* Someone will get short-changed. Someone will suffer. The human body can't be pushed that hard. It will eventually break. And the ultimate loser is usually that little fellow who stands in the doorway sucking his thumb and wondering why everybody is in such a hurry.

Mrs. Hull: There are few things more frustrating than

a never-ending to-do list . . . where you crowd so many responsibilities into a day that you can't handle any of them properly. Some of you will remember that this problem was discussed repeatedly at the Continental Congress on the Family, which was held in St. Louis in 1975. Jim [Dobson, Jr.] was one of the speakers. Did any others of you attend?

Dr. Cunningham: Yes, my wife and I were there.

Mrs. Hull: The purpose for the conference was to confront the same kinds of issues we will be discussing here and seek solutions to them. During one of the evening sessions, Dr. Howard Hendricks presented an audiovisual impression of the song "Cat's in the Cradle." The film dramatized a father who was too busy to get acquainted with his own son. He was always hoping to spend some time with his family, but "there were planes to catch and bills to pay." The son grew up and was too busy to visit his lonely father. It was a terribly emotional film.

Dr. Cunningham: Connie and I were sitting towards the front, and to dilute some of my own guilt, I looked around. There were several thousand people in the auditorium, and it looked as though everyone was in tears. These were Christian leaders. They weren't only weeping for families in their churches, they were identifying with their *own* families. The pressures are affecting us all.

Mrs. Hull: And the pressures are greatest for the mothers of toddlers who are trying to hold down full-time jobs and still meet the unending demands of motherhood. Once their kids get in school, the nature of maternal "homework" changes, somewhat.

Dr. Wiseman: I think you have some hope of selling the idea of mothers staying home if you are talking about the period of their childrens' preschool years.

14

Dr. Dobson, Jr.: Yes, one definition of maturity is the ability to postpone gratification. I don't see motherhood as a lifetime obligation because childhood passes so quickly, anyway. I think it should be seen as a temporary but vitally important responsibility. What could be more significant than taking a little life and molding it and shaping it and guiding it during those vulnerable years . . . teaching it to love the God that we love and preparing it for a life of responsible adulthood? That's worth a sacrifice, certainly.

Dr. Wiseman: That is valid.

Dr. Cunningham: But we can't ignore various income levels of the people who will read what we are saying today. I can hear someone mumbling, "Sure, it's easy to say, 'Wives shouldn't work,' when you can maintain the good life on one salary. It's another thing when there isn't enough money to go around." In most cases the issue is not whether or not a woman wants a career or a different role. For many people, the decision to work is dictated by pure economic consideration.

Mrs. Hull: I'm sure that's true.

Dr. Wiseman: I agree with that. I know many ministers, for example, who are maintained in the pastorate by the economic support of their wives.

Mr. Davis: That's terrible, Neil. It shouldn't be necessary. Paul, did your wife work when you were in a small church?

Dr. Cunningham: No, we started our ministry on a salary of $55.00 a week, and we agreed from the beginning that Connie was not going to work. We didn't put anybody else down who did it differently. But we had preschool children and felt that she should be home with them. She didn't work when I made $55.00 a week, and she doesn't work now. But I think we have to say something to our readers in terms of priorities. Yeah, it *is* easy to tell families to sacrifice and scrimp so mothers can stay home with the kids. But society puts so much pressure on us to live a certain way. Is there any way that we can help people to be able to live with that kind of decision? When a neighbor has two cars and you have none, and he has air conditioning and you are sweltering, it takes courage to say, "It's more important to me to have my wife at home."

Mrs. Hull: My husband has influenced me a lot in this area. Here's what he helped me see: In our day, many women live a long time after their children are gone. If God allows me to live, I may have 30 or more years to enjoy the freedom that will come when my job as a mother is over. I can tell you that I don't want to have those years marked by regrets like those I have seen in so many older women. They say, "If I had just done this or that, things would have been different." They seem so guilty and whip themselves every day. For me, it was almost a selfish conclusion that led me to say, "I'm going to do the very best job I can now, so I can enjoy the carefree years ahead without remorse and regret."

Rev. Dobson, Sr.: That's a healthy attitude, too, because it helps parents turn loose of their children as they grow and mature. To say to yourself, in other words, "I have this parental responsibility now, but it will soon be over. When that change comes, I'll have a different kind of life." And underlying all this is the Christian principle "He that will lose his life shall find it," which gives us an inside track if we believe.

Mrs. Hull: It has worked in my family. It also relates to another biblical principle: "It is more blessed to give than to receive." Even in response to my husband, when I submit myself to him and try to meet his needs, he gives the same support back to me. He shows me he cares about my concerns and my feeling and my needs. And I am always the winner. That's the way I see my children. They are expensive, but I get back everything I put into them.

Dr. Cunningham: Yes, it's a symbiotic relationship: Husbands and wives should meet *each other's* needs. For me, there isn't any place in the world I'd rather go than home; and that may sound redundant or corny, but there are obviously men who have little interest in being with their families. My love for my home is due in large measure to my wife, Connie, who is a registered nurse and a tremendous person who could have insisted on a career of her own. She was teaching nursing while I was in seminary, and she obviously had a bright future in her profession.

But she decided one day that her greatest contribution to ongoing generations (not only for our own children, but to other kids as well) could be made by assisting me in my ministry and helping me to achieve what God wanted for my life. She concluded that she could satisfy her needs by pouring herself into our home, making it a place of repair and refuge and harbor . . . a place of love and order. That's why I can't wait to come home because she acts like she is glad that I'm there. And because she has so ordered things that I don't have to resolve a lot of conflicts that I might have otherwise had to handle. And that's not necessarily an easy thing to do.

But we have in our ministry a "team" concept, where Connie is definitely a part of my real world, and I'm a part of her real world, and we communicate on that basis. She's my equal; she is my source of human strength. All of this makes going home a joy and a privilege for me. But now I have an equally important contribution to make in that relationship too, in that I try to make her feel as special as she really is. I try to make her aware of how much I need her, and when I achieve a success, it's her success too. And not in some saccharine, superficial way, but she actually feels a part of me.

Rev. Dobson, Sr.: Does she ever express to you a sense of frustration that she has given up what she might have been professionally in order to accept the role of wife and mother?

Dr. Cunningham: The answer is in two parts. She does express frustration to me sometimes because I get very much out of hand. I get fatigued and over-worked like everyone else. There are times when I am not the father I need to be or the husband I need to be; and when those times occur, she tells me. We have that kind of openness and mutual responsibility in the relationship which permits us to express our genuine feelings, even if they are not always positive.

But now for the other part of the answer. No, Connie is still interested in her profession and she keeps vitally involved, but at this point she says that her emotional needs are being met through the family that she is so much a part of. There are outlets. I mean in teaching and speaking. She has a group of about 35-40 young married couples that she teaches. She had a very successful Bible study class in our immediate neighborhood . . . activities like that. So there are many creative things that she is involved in.

Rev. Dobson, Sr.: The involvement you mentioned is more or less supplementary to your responsibility; but how about the nostalgic longing for a fulfilling career in her own right?

Dr. Cunningham: Well, she says she is totally fulfilled in the career that she has, and I believe she means it.

Dr. Dobson, Jr.: That's the primary message of my book. If husbands will do the jobs God gave them . . . loving their wives as their own flesh, with all that that means . . . then wives will be much more comfortable in accepting their supportive roles with enthusiasm and self-esteem.

Mrs. Hull: How can a man learn what his wife needs from him?

Dr. Dobson, Jr.: Shirley taught me what her needs were in the early days of our marriage . . . not by wagging her finger in my face, nor by henpecking or browbeating me, but by explaining her feelings to me during times of communication and understanding. I think women need to do that. First, of course, they have to have a husband who's listening. But one of the reasons that I was listening to Shirley was because she was also doing something valuable for me. Right from the beginning, my young wife said to me in so many ways: "I believe in you. I'm really glad to be part of your team, because I know that God is going to do good things with 'our lives.'" She gave me such confidence through her approach that it was easy for me to give love back to her.

Mr. Davis: Beverly and I came through a severe crisis over this matter of roles and careers about 10 years ago. She was in graduate school at USC, and she was told by the head of the Department of Piano that she had great capabilities as a pianist. Maybe she wouldn't have been a concert pianist, but she definitely had what it took to excel. Her career became more important than anything else. At the same time, I was anything but a model husband, and our marriage was steadily disintegrating. God began to deal with Beverly first . . . to speak to her from the Book of Ephesians on the matter of wives submitting to their husbands.

She entered into a kind of union with God which made it possible for her to submit to my leadership . . . even though she was probably more capable of leading than I was. Her responsiveness to God had a dramatic impact on our marriage. Then the Lord began to put pressure on me to be a better husband and devote myself to Beverly's needs. We both obeyed His leadings, and He healed our home.

Dr. Hernandez: How did Beverly feel about forfeiting her career, just like that?

Mr. Davis: I don't think that you can have the allurement of the world and have people telling you how great you are without feeling a loss when you give up your dreams. All of a sudden you're a mother and housewife and you're home washing dirty diapers and doing dishes and cleaning the house and preparing lunches and this type of thing. It couldn't possibly be as glamorous as playing the piano or whatever. So Beverly went through a process of adjustment until she came to realize that being a mother and a good wife and teaching our children were the most important things in her life.

When she came face-to-face with eternal values, she began to see herself in a very different light. Now God is helping me to reinforce that. And I can say that to her, "Honey, I love you and I think that the job you're doing with our children is so fantastic, and I'm so proud of our kids and what you're doing for them." She is being successful; she is doing the best job that she can do as a person, and she's finding it fulfilling. That's exciting to me!

Dr. Wiseman: I'm not second-guessing what you said. That's a beautiful concept. The only place I'm having some problems is with your use of the word *submission*. What do you mean by it?

Mr. Davis: Well, let me define it in reference to my own situation, again. Beverly and I had a kind of power struggle before our spiritual renewal. When we disagreed on an issue, we either fought about it until one of us won, or we took turns having our way, etc. In regard to spending money, we were both teaching school, so she spent her check and I spent mine. But I can tell you that we were living in a veritable hell on earth . . . even though no one knew it. Not even our parents were aware of the trouble we were in. It was only the pressure of the church and our basic Christian teachings that kept us from separating.

God began to show Beverly, first, that He wanted her to submit to my authority in areas of spiritual life, emotional life, our homelife, etc. And I mean *submit.* Now, if we don't like that word, maybe we can change it; but the Bible says, "Wives, submit yourselves unto your own husbands." To Beverly, this meant that the Lord wanted her to bring herself under my authority which He wanted to establish in our relationship. And the change that occurred was miraculous.

Dr. Wiseman: You are saying what I thought you meant.

Mr. Davis: And you're saying that you don't like it.

Dr. Wiseman: No, I don't. There is no way I could find a meaningful relationship with that kind of setup in my marriage. My wife has to be my equal.

Mr. Davis: That's not what I meant.

Dr. Wiseman: There is no way that I could think of my wife submitting physically, spiritually, and emotionally the way you said a moment ago. Neither of us could live with that.

Mr. Davis: All I can tell you is that this reversal in our relationship brought Beverly into a place where she was not trying to change me. She would allow God to bring changes in my life. There were many things about my personality and our life together that needed to be improved, but I rebelled at the idea of my wife changing me just as she rebels at the idea of me trying to change her. When she turned it over to God, *He* did the rearranging.

Rev. Dobson, Sr.: Neil, why don't you give your definition of the scripture in Eph. 5:22-23 that Jim [Davis] mentioned, "You wives must submit to your husbands' leadership in the same way you submit to the Lord. For a husband is in charge of his wife in the same way Christ is in charge of His body the Church" (TLB).

Dr. Wiseman: I don't think it means that the husband is necessarily the boss of the home, and what he says goes without negotiating with his wife.

Mr. Davis: What do you think it means?

Dr. Wiseman: I think it means that he takes spiritual leadership.

Mr. Davis: And doesn't spiritual leadership then pervade every other avenue of Christian thinking in a home?

Dr. Wiseman: Yes, except that my wife has the same spiritual goals that I have. Sometimes her ideas are better than mine. Sometimes I ought to be in a position of negotiating and thinking through an issue with her, because her idea may be better than mine. Why is it that she is to submit to me?

Mr. Davis: That's not what I'm talking about here in reference to submission.

Dr. Dobson, Jr.: I think we need to work this through to some understanding, because so many Christians today seem to be struggling with the meaning of submission.

Dr. Wiseman: The thing that's hard to live with is that just because you're a male, you're in a higher position in the sight of God than a female, and I can't buy that.

Mrs. Hull: To me, submission means that if my husband and I ever have a difference of opinion or a conflict about something which we cannot resolve or negotiate, then we go his way. He always listens to me, and many times I can convince him and he changes his mind. But if we both feel strongly about something, I yield. I don't know how else to describe it.

Dr. Dobson, Jr.: I sense some difficulty with the word *equal*. You said that your wife was equal to you, Neil.

Dr. Wiseman: Yes.

Dr. Dobson, Jr.: Well, that word has two different connotations. One refers to being equal in worth and status and importance and dignity.

Dr. Wiseman: Yes. All right, that's where I'm coming from.

Dr. Dobson, Jr.: I think Jim [Davis] would agree that he and his wife are equal in that respect. I certainly feel that way about my wife. But equal does not mean equivalent; you can be equal in worth and have different functions and different roles. Aarlie really hit it, I think, in terms of the real meaning of submission. It's not that a wife becomes a child or a nonperson, never expressing an opinion or a disagreement. I want all the input my wife will give me. I want her to express her views without reservation, because I don't have all the answers. But on those occasions when we can't compromise or harmonize our points of view, she yields to my decision.

Mr. Davis: If she doesn't, you'll have the chaos that the Western world is experiencing. There can be only one final decision maker in a home—the husband—even though he listens to his wife and is influenced by her.

Dr. Hernandez: I want to comment here because I really think we're getting to the nitty-gritty of this problem. Marriage, as I see it, is a kind of corporation. Two persons who put in the same amount of money are equal partners in a corporation, but in order for that business to function efficiently, one becomes the senior partner and the other one, perhaps, becomes the treasurer. And in that fashion, the corporation functions.

Or let me give another analogy, even though it may be a bit clinical. In conception, there is a sperm and an ova which are equally important in order for the progeny . . . the future generations . . . to be produced. But it's the sperm that determines whether the baby will be a boy or girl. You can't have life without both contributors. That's essentially the kind of relationship that husbands and wives have. If we don't have some kind of functional structure in our marriages, then there will be trouble in the relationship; we will have "unholy deadlock" instead of holy wedlock. Functionally there has to be a system. This doesn't mean that a wife is a doormat for her husband to dominate.

Dr. Wiseman: But that is exactly what happens in many cases. The guy out there who already has his wife ground under his heel says, "Uh-huh, it says right there in that Book that I'm going to be the boss here."

Dr. Hernandez: Well, you also have to emphasize the spiritual concept that husbands are to love their wives as they love their own selves. A wife is part of her husband's body. A Christian husband who is following the biblical pattern wouldn't do anything to injure his mate any more than he would injure himself. And therefore, unless he is masochistic, he loves himself too much to cause pain to someone who is part of him.

Dr. Wiseman: Okay, if you use *submission* the way we are using it here—my wife is in submission to me, but I am to love her like Christ loves the Church—then it is reasonable.

Dr. Cunningham: I call this a balanced equation. "So husbands, love your wives as Christ loved the church." How did He love the Church? He was the suffering Servant. And this was perhaps most beautifully pictured after Jesus and His disciples had made a journey of many miles. They had been on this sweaty, dusty trip, and Jesus said, "Bring Me the basin; bring Me the towel. This is how I love the Church; this is how I serve the Church; I wash their feet. I accept the servant's role." That was the model of loving leadership.

So in applying that to the husband-and-wife relationship, a man who is functioning as Christ intended is continuously seeking ways to serve his wife and to care for his children. Now what wife wouldn't want to submit herself to that kind of man who has only her highest good as his intention? But the dude you're talking about who's grinding his wife under his heel is certainly not implementing a balanced equation. And neither is that a biblical understanding. He has made the Bible say what he wanted it to say.

Dr. Wiseman: If there's a clear understanding of this "balanced equation" concept, then it is a reasonable approach to a marital relationship. But the idea that my maleness makes me somehow 5 degrees or 50 degrees better than my wife, is, I think, counterproductive to a good marriage relationship.

Dr. Cunningham: I couldn't agree with you more. When I first got into this *submission* concept, I couldn't conceive of asking my wife to submit to me. But I became conscious of the fact that she had been submitting to me all along. She was implementing Dave's concept of a good corporation. The buck has to stop somewhere. How do you resolve a problem in your home when you each have your own opinions and no one will compromise? Somebody has to have the responsibility for making the ultimate decision, and it would appear, by God's Word, that this functional role belongs to the husband.

Rev. Dobson, Sr.: It belongs to the husband; but if he's smart, there will be times when he will pass it to his wife. I learned a long time ago that my wife is definitely more intelligent in some areas than I am (and maybe in all areas). But I've learned it's to my good to put some questions to her and let her solve them, because she handles certain assignments better than I do.

Dr. Cunningham: The more enlightened Christian writers are expressing this egalitarian approach. To some degree, there should be an interchangeability of roles. A lot of women are smarter than men, for example, when it comes to handling finances. Because you are a male does not mean you *have* to control the money. I say it is a wise thing for a woman to do whatever she and her husband agree is best for the home, regardless of what the role calls for. And for the man not to feel as though his ego is threatened or frustrated by this interchangeability.

Dr. Hernandez: That's true. A good corporation president will listen to his associates before making decisions. He will listen carefully. One time I got a card from my wife at the office (this was about two or three years ago). She sent me a lovely card and she wrote on it, "Are you listening?" I think there are times when we husbands need to tune in to our wives.

Dr. Cunningham: I agree very much with Neil that the "submission issue" has been overstated in some of the Christian literature today, and I disagree with many popular opinions on the subject. I can accept the kind of concept we have been working out here.

Rev. Dobson, Sr.: This reminds me of something I said to my wife not long ago. I think it was on our wedding anniversary. I said, "Myrtle, we have been married 42 years. One thing is certain. Living together for all those years hasn't made a Dillingham out of me or a Dobson out of you."

Mrs. Hull: And you wouldn't want it to, would you?

Rev. Dobson, Sr.: No. The biblical concept doesn't go so far as to destroy personhood. My wife and I bang an idea back and forth from such different viewpoints that it'll never get past both of us unless it's pretty good. We have opposite opinions on nearly everything, but we can eventually work them out!

Dr. Dobson, Jr.: I agree with Paul and Neil that we've been hearing a distorted concept of submission during the past six or eight years. But my fear is that we will send the pendulum back to the other extreme again, ignoring the real meaning of Ephesians 5.

Dr. Wiseman: I don't want to do that.

Dr. Dobson, Jr.: There is obviously a divine plan lying between the two extreme positions.

Mrs. Hull: Another essential part of that divine plan involves a lifetime *commitment* to your mate. Young people are being told today that male-female relationships work best as a day-to-day arrangement, but that attitude almost guarantees the failure of a marriage.

Dr. Cunningham: I heard of a wedding ceremony the

other day where bride and bridegroom each said, "I pledge myself to you for as long as I love you." This was the extent of their commitment.

Mr. Davis: Which might last through the ceremony.

Mrs. Hull: Definitely not the first night.

Dr. Dobson, Jr.: The honeymoon would wipe it out.

Dr. Wiseman: Like Aarlie said, basically and fundamentally, married life is a commitment of two people to each other *for life*, and all of the other good things grow out of that stable relationship.

Rev. Dobson, Sr.: Well, God would not have commanded a husband and wife to enter into a permanent relationship of love if it were not possible. He would not have demanded it. It *is* possible. We have to get this across to little children and help them prepare for it. This concept of a lifetime commitment was so thoroughly ingrained in me *during childhood* that later when I entered marriage it was with an unshakable resolve to make it last. In fact, I expressed this to my wife before we were married, many years ago. Here is the substance of what I said to her. I didn't state it exactly like this, but in recalling it I have put in formal language the exact thought I conveyed at the time:

"I want you to understand and be fully aware of my feelings concerning the marriage covenant which we are about to enter. I have been taught at my mother's knee and in harmony with the Word of God, that the marriage vows are inviolable; and by entering into them, I am binding myself absolutely and for life. The idea of estrangement from you through divorce for any reason at all (though God allows one) will never at any time be allowed to enter into my thinking. I'm not naive in this. On the contrary, I am fully aware of the possibility, unlikely as it now appears, that *mutual incompatibility* or other unforeseen circumstances could result in extreme mental suffering. If such becomes the case, I am resolved (for my part) to accept it as a consequence of the commitment I am now making, and to bear it, if necessary, to the end of our lives together. I have loved you dearly as a sweetheart and will continue to love you as my wife; *but* over and above that, I love you with a Christian love that demands that I never react in any way toward you that would jeopardize your prospects of entering heaven, which is the supreme objective of both our lives. I pray that God himself will make our affection for one another perfect and eternal."

I think if you go into marriage with that attitude . . . well, it's lasted 42 years for us.

Dr. Wiseman: That's terrific! That's the stuff that stable families are made of.

(Entire group expressed agreement with the statement and appreciation for the way it was phrased.)

Mrs. Hull: I wish we could also teach our kids the concept that love is more than a warm feeling.

Dr. Cunningham: Every young woman or man about to get married should know that there will definitely be periods of dissatisfaction . . . that feelings oscillate. Emotions aren't very dependable in anybody, even in the most stable relationship. There will be times when your determination must be solidly entrenched, even if your feelings are bland or negative.

Dr. Dobson, Jr.: Yes, and they ought to know about the compromises which marriage requires. Take my situation, for example. My wife can't go to sleep at night unless she is snuggled up to my back. What that means in practical terms is that I spend most of the night sleeping on the left side of my body. That has gone on for 16 years, now, and I'm beginning to flatten out on one side! And I'm sure my heart and liver and the rest of the internal organs are gradually drifting toward the left hemisphere!

Rev. Dobson, Sr.: What a sacrifice!

Mr. Davis: That is "commitment" at its most basic level!

The Masculine Role

Mr. Davis: I wish we had an opportunity to spend more time discussing the latter part of Ephesians 5. There are some strong statements there about the responsibilities of husbands and fathers. At lunchtime, we were talking about Derek Prince's recording on "Fatherhood." In that tape, Prince says that the American husband is a "renegade male." He has reneged on his God-given responsibilities to provide leadership in his home . . . parental leadership . . . spiritual leadership . . . financial leadership . . . and to love his wife as his own flesh. He has abandoned many aspects of the job assigned to him by the Scriptures.

Dr. Wiseman: Ephesians 5 stresses this concept of acceptance and warmth and love to be shown by husbands . . . and it's in that context that submission of a wife becomes practical.

Mr. Davis: That's right. Jim [Dobson, Jr.] emphasized this point in *What Wives Wish . . .*, and a similar perspective is contained in Charlie Shedd's excellent book *Letters to Philip*. They both described how vitally important it is for a man to treat his wife lovingly— with respect and tenderness. This is often not happening, and it explains why so many women are agitated today. There is a widespread feeling of loneliness and isolation . . . of not being a part of a husband's work or not being included in his problems or his decisions or his world. And when success comes to him, she doesn't share it. When his needs are being met, hers are not. We need to reestablish the idea of being a team and being "one." Not just "one in the spirit," but being one in the physical and emotional and the romantic. But busy men find it difficult to establish those relationships, because it takes time to develop *any* friendship.

Dr. Dobson, Jr.: That frustration is often expressed to me by women in counseling . . . that there is no romantic attraction between themselves and their husbands . . . there is no sense of partnership, no feeling of cohesiveness or of understanding. Instead, each family member goes his own way and does his own job but feels like no one cares. No one understands. I'm convinced that men can tolerate that condition of loneliness better than women, because women are the ones who are more often depressed and disenchanted.

Rev. Dobson, Sr.: Are you saying, then, that husbands and fathers hold the keys to meaningful family life?

Dr. Dobson, Jr.: Each member of the family has an important role to play; but as Derek Prince said, men have apparently been ordained by God for leadership in the home. And when they are too busy to fulfill that responsibility, then everyone suffers. Let me state it more strongly: If the family has a chance of surviving, it will be necessary for husbands to begin to place their wives and children at the highest level of their priorities.

Rev. Dobson, Sr.: Why do you feel so many are not doing that now?

Dr. Dobson, Jr.: Because men tend to meet their needs for self-esteem through their work. Therefore, it is easy for a man to become engulfed by his outside responsibilities, pouring himself into his job six and seven days a week. Men like this have been called "workaholics," which is a fitting title. They are literally addicted to their work. And when they do finally come home from the office, they're too tired to do anything but watch television. One woman said her husband watched so many athletic events on TV that if she divorced him, he wouldn't know it unless they announced it on "Wide World of Sports"!

Dr. Wiseman: The question is, How can we turn that situation around so that a man can meet his needs for self-esteem through his wife and family?

Dr. Dobson, Jr.: That's the goal, but it requires a complete reorientation of masculine values and attitudes in most homes. Whether it is cultural or genetic, I don't know, but I have observed that most men look outside their families for self-worth. This explains why they are so depressed and upset when fired or laid off from their jobs.

Mrs. Hull: I don't think I agree with that. My husband meets his needs within our family. For instance, he loves to go to parent-teacher conferences to hear how well the kids are doing in school. He gets great personal satisfaction and an ego boost from things like that.

Dr. Dobson, Jr.: He obviously has his values in the right place, Aarlie, and I hope the rest of us here are doing the same. But in my dealing with families across the United States, I would have to say that your home situation is not typical of the majority. Maybe it's the way we're taught; maybe the false values are drilled into us from childhood. For whatever reason, the greatest kicks in life for millions of men come from business and professional successes, and not from Johnny's grades or the stability of their marriages. When men get together and they're comparing credentials and getting acquainted for the first time, do they say, "Well, you know my wife is really healthy and happy, and my son is doing great in baseball?" No, they say, "I'm the president of so and so, and I manage this, and I own that." That's where masculine self-esteem is rooted. I think we need to call this fact to the attention of Christian fathers and make a concerted effort to teach them that those social values are wrong. Jobs are important, but families are more important.

Dr. Hernandez: I think Jim's point is valid. I know from the couples I see in my practice that most husbands find their happiness and joy and self-image and self-worth, not in their homes, but outside of them. This is one reason people are so miserable today. Husbands and wives and children are looking outside the home for the resources they need. There's no real stability in that. Fifty years ago, people took great pride in their large families. A son or a daughter was an asset and not a liability. Fathers were proud to have a son to bring up, train, and have him take over his business. Now we have a complete reversal of that viewpoint. We must reestablish the idea that the home is a place of support and love . . . a refuge where we can recharge our batteries, physically and mentally, and not depend so heavily on the competitive outside world.

Mr. Davis: A man can derive tremendous pleasure from seeing his wife being successful and being fulfilled, from seeing his children being healthy and normal and successful in school, and from feeling like they are making a contribution to God. My dad was (and is) that way. He never had the chance to get a formal education, and he has gotten most of his satisfaction in life from watching his kids grow up and be successful. He believed that his greatest opportunity to make a contribution to God and to society was by doing a good job as a husband and father.

Dr. Hernandez: It's beautiful when a father cares like that, but again, men like your father and Aarlie's husband are exceptions. I have even had to agonize through some personal crises in my own life before being willing to reorder my priorities. Look at the men in our local church and you'll see what the fellows *really* care about. I mean just look at them. I could run through the names of a dozen or more men . . . good friends of mine . . . who have shared this problem with me personally. Their businesses are their whole lives. If we can help men deal with this one error . . . this one failing . . . then our effort to create this book will not be in vain.

Mrs. Hull: In all fairness, I should tell you of some of the dynamics that brought my husband to this point. His values weren't always so noble. He is a very aggressive man and wanted to be on top—and he usually was (or was close to it). And as a result, when he finished his orthopedic residency, he chose a location where he felt he would have an immediately successful practice. He was very busy from the beginning and never had to search for patients. Within one year he had a partner, and four months later they were both doing as well as anyone. So what was left for him to accomplish? Big deal! He had reached his goal and it didn't satisfy him.

He began to see that even success in medicine was not enough "ego stuff" for him. He needed something more, and he began to realize that the things he wanted most could be found in good relationships within our family. The success he had worked for years and years to achieve wasn't as satisfying as being loved and needed by me and the children. But then I wonder if he would still be striving if he had not first achieved those outside goals and accomplishments.

Dr. Hernandez: That speaks to me. In my personal life, I achieved a modicum of financial security, and I was surrounded by all kinds of life insurance policies and investments. For practical purposes, I could have retired at a young age and lived pretty comfortably. But then I discovered one day that I was facing death, and all my medical associates . . . all my expert professional colleagues at the University of Southern California . . . could not take care of my physical problem. My money, my investments—*nothing* could save me from the predicament that I found myself in. I can tell you that my priorities really went topsy-turvy, and I began to realize that my life had to amount to more than success and investments and advancement of my private practice in medicine.

I had to go through that difficulty. Your husband, Aarlie, obviously learned the same lesson without having to go through such a devastating experience. He understood the concept at the right moment. That's the way we should do it. We shouldn't wait until pressed by the edge of death or hardship in order to come to that reality. The beauty of the Christian life is that it *does* satisfy, and the principles on which the family is based can be trusted to govern our lives. I wish more persons could learn to reorder their priorities without having to face death or disaster to put "first things first."

Phsyical and Emotional Distinctions Between Males and Females

Dr. Hernandez: I'd like to return to Jim's point that equal worth between men and women does not mean that they have equivalent functions. We've been hearing so much nonsense from the Women's Liberation Movement, and elsewhere, telling us that males and females are identical except for reproductive functioning. That is ridiculous. Our differences are much more profound that the obvious genital characteristics. We are unique electro-chemically, emotionally, sexually, and anatomically. And these differences play an important role in everything we do.

Dr. Dobson, Jr.: Some of those influences are so subtle that we aren't aware of them. Did you know, for example, that adolescent males typically carry their school books in one arm at their sides, while females usually cradle them to their breasts in both arms, as they would an infant? There are many behaviors like this which apparently reflect the influence of our sexual and reproductive roles.

Dr. Hernandez: It is foolish to try to deny the existence of these influences.

Dr. Dobson, Jr.: Dave, how would you respond to the catch phrase "Anatomy is destiny," which is resented so fiercely by the Women's Movement? In other words, because a woman is female, is she locked into a prescribed role and has no choice and no way out?

Dr. Hernandez: I don't feel that anyone is locked in, but everything that we do is related to sex, one way or the other. The way we dress, the way I relate with Neil, the way I relate to others. I identify as a male. The way my wife identifies with another person . . . everything reflects our self-concept as man or woman. There's no question that this influences our entire lives. So in that sense, anatomy plays an important role in our destinies. But on the other hand, free choice carries enormous influence, too.

Dr. Cunningham: Dave, I think it would be helpful if you would provide some scientific substantiation to what you were saying. You know, I preach messages on Mother's Day and Father's Day, relating some of the basic differences between males and females. But I usually get a reaction from someone . . . a hot letter from somebody who says, "How dare you infer that there are innate differences!" Would you delineate the specific ways the sexes are unique and how those characteristics influence us?

Dr. Hernandez: Well, women are so delicately constructed. The Lord designed such a beautiful system that it is almost overwhelming. That's why I'm in obstetrics and gynecology. I have such deep respect for the procreative process in women, and it is very distressing for me to see how it has been degraded in our society during the past decade.

But to answer your question, let me give an example of how men are different from women. Let's suppose a young lady has just had a car accident. It may frighten her so badly that she could stop menstruating for four to six months. Why? Because of the delicate balance between the hypothalamus and the pituitary gland. As some of you know, the pituitary gland is situated right at the base of the brain. It has been called the "master gland" of the body because it controls practically everything, particularly in women. It releases hormones which influence the adrenal glands, ovarian function, thyroid glands, breast development, and all endocrine functioning. The pituitary keeps all these organs in operation, just like clockwork. It's a beautiful process.

But this master gland is subject to influences too, particularly from the hypothalamus. It is located just above the pituitary and is often called "the seat of the emotions." these two organs are integrated by nerve connections and by secretions, so that anything which affects one usually has an impact on the other. This is how a woman's emotions get translated into physical phenomena. You see, a psychological jolt is received by the hypothalamus and passed along to the pituitary. For example, if a woman questions her femininity, she may not ovulate for months or even years. She has a block between the hypothalamus and the pituitary. If she becomes extremely nervous or tense, she may experience what we call anorexia nervousa, which can eliminate both menstrual periods and ovulation. Or if she has doubts about her capacity to meet the desires of her husband or the needs of her children, this may also affect her capacity.

There are so many things that will influence this very delicate balance. If a husband comes home from work and immediately says to her, "Let's go upstairs," and demands that she have sex at that particular moment, she is likely to be inorgasmic. She is simply not geared that way. A man can have a fight with his wife and even beat her up and then proceed to have sexual intercourse with her. He may climax and have satisfaction, but she is most unlikely to achieve an orgasm. And we wonder, "What's wrong with her?" Well, she's wired differently, that's all. She's responding differently. Men and women are not the same.

Dr. Cunningham: Contrast that, now, with corresponding biochemistry in males.

Dr. Hernandez: Males don't experience this monthly cyclic phenomenon, so their system is entirely different. For instance, it takes a male 70 to 90 days to form sperm. So his cycle is completely different. He doesn't have a regular fluctuation.

Dr. Cunningham: But isn't there an interrelationship between his hypothalamus to pituitary?

Dr. Hernandez: Yes. But males don't have the very delicate mechanisms related to the monthly cyclic phenomenon. In the female, there is a feedback mechanism to the pituitary, whereby the ovaries produce estrogens and progestins. These hormones help keep the psyche in order. The male is not geared that way because his system is designed for an entirely different purpose. We have a more steady hormonal output. This is why I'm saying that women are very vulnerable to all kinds of emotional circumstances. A husband can sometimes depress his wife simply by walking into the house and keeping his mouth shut . . . acting like he doesn't want to talk to her. She has been waiting to talk to him all day long, and she's anxious to look at him and talk to him. And of course, like Jim said in his book *What Wives Wish* . . ., the first hour we're home sets the tone for the whole evening. But wives are very tender and very delicate and we need to understand that as men, we husbands should hold our wives with such gentleness and respect and love. This is the way God intended a marital relationship to function, and His intention is reflected in our unique bodies.

Mrs. Hull: Dave, don't most sexual problems result from a breakdown in interpersonal relationships, rather than from organic malfunctions? Would you like to comment on that?

Dr. Hernandez: Yes. You know, I have husbands and wives coming into my office who wonder why the woman has been orgasmic for the last few years. The husband is just going to pieces because now somehow his maleness has been challenged, too, because he can't bring her across. If you begin to explore the matter, the basic problem is not sexual; it results from the fact that *relationships* have been broken. I tell you that in the last 12 to 14 years that I've been dealing with sexual dysfunctions, I think less than 2 percent of my patients have had genuine organic problems. Almost all of them have had emotional problems and lack of communication between husband and wife. Their relationship disintegrated and this has affected her responsiveness and eventually his. This is a key reason why marriages are falling apart.

And now with the sexual revolution, even more demands are coming. Men are trying to experiment sexually. They go to their wives and ask them to perform some kind of sexual gymnastics because at lunchtime their buddies were reading *Playboy* and exchanging ideas of what new games they could try. And they go home and demand those same performances from their wives, but the poor lady is frustrated. She doesn't know what's happening, but all of a sudden many new demands have been placed upon her. And then she comes rushing to me and says, "What's happening? What's wrong with me? Am I going crazy? I'm going to lose my husband!" She feels terribly threatened because if she doesn't meet her husband's demands, he may leave her. These are some of the reasons families are falling apart.

Mr. Davis: Worldwide.

Dr. Hernandez: That's right.

Dr. Dobson, Jr.: David, will you elaborate on some of the things we talked about before? I believe you said you had seen an increase in the physical disorders that are directly linked to stress, such as hypertension, ulcers, and so on, which seem to increase in frequency as the sexual revolution has grown.

Dr. Hernandez: Well, there's no question that this is occurring. I have a patient, for example, who has been married for 30 years. Her husband has come home recently and said, "I've been hearing an awful lot about orgasm and I'm concerned that you have never had one. If I can't satisfy you, I am going to search somewhere else." This lady who had never experienced orgasm, and in fact had never missed it, went into a severe depression. She was sure that something was terribly wrong with her. She is now about 45 or 50 years of age. (She was married quite young.) Her children are in college and now her concentration has been shifted from them to her husband, but she is faced with the possibility of him leaving her. She has already lost her children and now her husband is threatening to leave. No one really needs her. This is the woman who comes into my office in severe depression wanting, hoping, that I can find something organically wrong so that I can correct it. This is the kind of situation that's created by the concentration on sex today.

Another example is seen with the husband who is trying to prove his manhood. He is demanding that he and his wife have sexual intercourse once or twice a day. She loves her husband so much and she says to me, "My husband thinks about nothing but sex, but I can't keep up with him. Is something wrong with me?" That kind of emotional pressure causes physical disorders to occur.

Consider, also, the wife who comes in with a fertility problem. This can create havoc in a family, not only for the wife, but for the husband, as well. What I'm saying is that a society's attitude toward sex has the power to help sustain a marriage or blow it apart . . . or even make the difference between health and disease.

Dr. Dobson, Jr.: Dave, I wonder if you have observed what I have seen in the last two or three years. I've counseled an increasing number of *men* who express sexual frustration. I haven't heard those complaints as commonly in the past. It would appear that the sexual emancipation of women has put some males under pressure for the first time.

Dr. Hernandez: I've observed that, too. As women make sexual demands on their husbands, the pressure to perform creates new anxieties in males.

Dr. Dobson, Jr.: I got a letter from a Christian fellow the other day and he said, "I appreciated your new book and the chapter on sex, but how come Christian books on the subject of sex always take the point of view that the husbands are clamoring for sex and their wives are cold? We have the opposite problem in our marriage and no one writes about it."

Dr. Hernandez: This is another area which we are going to be hearing even more about in the next two or three years.

Mrs. Hull: My husband and I spoke on a college campus last year about sex, marriage, and related topics. To our surprise, the guys told us that girls had become much more aggressive. We had been making the point that girls come on slower, but the fellows said, "Don't tell us that. The girls are the assertive ones now."

Dr. Hernandez: It is a fact. Behavior is changing, I believe, because of the messages we are getting from television. People are experimenting with things that girls wouldn't have tried during the 1960s.

Mrs. Hull: One female student said, "I think it is a greater sin for a married couple who hate each other to have sex than it is for an unmarried couple who love each other dearly."

Dr. Dobson, Jr.: What did you tell her, Aarlie?

Mrs. Hull: I said, "You're making a big mistake. God's moral laws can't be revised, simply because they don't seem modern to us. The Bible says, 'There is a way which seemeth right unto a man, but the end thereof are the ways of death.'"

Mr. Davis: Dave, will the increased sexual freedom and knowledge available to young people today lead to more successful sexual experiences in marriage?

Dr. Hernandez: Not necessarily. I'm concerned about the notion that being an "expert" in the bedroom will solve all our problems. The bedroom is a nice place to share very intimate relations in a home, but the 20 or 30 minutes spent in a physical encounter still leaves 23½ hours in the day to interact with one another on a personal level. Also, just knowing the sexual "tricks" and facts and positions doesn't automatically produce a meaningful sex life. The most important part of the entire process is the intimate relationship which they share. If the man and woman love each other deeply and are committed to making their partner happy, then they can learn the mechanics together.

Dr. Wiseman: That puts sex in its proper perspective.

Winning Children to Christ

Dr. Dobson, Jr.: We have focused our discusson on the roles of husbands and wives this morning, and about various influences on our homes. Perhaps we should talk now about children and our responsibilities as parents. Let's begin with the task of leading our children to Christ . . . which is the ultimate goal of parenthood, I believe.

Rev. Dobson, Sr.: I'm concerned about the fact that children too often are not part of the preaching ministries in their local churches. They need to hear preaching which is anointed by the Spirit of God, just like adults do. I would never have been willing to turn over the matter of the salvation of my children to a secondary officer in the church and never see them in the main service.

Dr. Dobson, Jr.: There is a good Sunday evening program specifically for children at our church, but I must admit that I have been undecided as to whether or not to let my kids attend it. It is difficult for them to sit through an adult service; but on the other hand, I agree that they need more than a "teaching ministry" such as in children's church. There is a place for inspired preaching.

Rev. Dobson, Sr.: I may be entirely off base here.

Dr. Cunningham: No, I don't think you are. In some places we have practically written our children right out of the mainstream of the church.

Rev. Dobson, Sr.: I know that I got many of my early religious impressions from being on the second row of the sanctuary where we always were when there was a revival meeting. And likely as not, we went to the altar at the end of the service, with our friends praying for us. "Teaching" is an entirely different form of ministry. Children need to be *converted*. And when that occurs, I want to be part of it.

Dr. Wiseman: Elaborate a bit on what you mean by that.

Rev. Dobson, Sr.: I want to be there, if my kid is seeking God and having spiritual trouble; I don't want somebody to merely tell me about it. I want to be where he is; I want to be praying for him.

Dr. Dobson, Jr.: I agree with that. I can remember services when I was a child that had a tremendous impact on me. There were times when the power of God was so strong that I could almost reach out and touch Him. I want my kids to see and feel those experiences, too.

Dr. Cunningham: I think it is a very valid point. We have a lot of watery Christian stuff going on in many instructional programs.

Mr. Davis: I think the scripture backs up Rev. Dobson. God's method of communicating the gospel is within a family context. The father is the high priest of the home . . . and he is largely responsible for the salvation of his own children. If he loses them, he can't point to the pastor of the church or the Sunday school teachers or the children's church coordinator or anyone else. I think this is *the* greatest responsibility given to parents—to communicate the gospel to their own children.

Dr. Dobson, Jr.: I have to admit that when my kids go to Sunday school every week, I don't know very much about what's going on there. I am so totally removed from it.

Rev. Dobson, Sr.: Isn't that contributing to the generation gap?

Dr. Dobson, Jr.: I think it puts us in different worlds spiritually unless we make an effort to bridge that gap.

Rev. Dobson, Sr.: How do children learn to behave in church if they never go there? No wonder so many don't attend church when they get older.

Mrs. Hull: Do you know how we solved this problem? The youngest child always get to sit and snuggle in Daddy's lap, and they love that.

Mr. Davis: My concern is not limited to what my children experience in church. I also want to guarantee that there is the proper spiritual tone in our home. The quality of family devotions is important, for example.

Dr. Dobson, Jr.: Most people need training in how to make family devotions meaningful. I was talking to a church leader a few years ago, and he related an incident that occurred with some of his fellow pastors. They were in a kind of seminar and were asked to describe the most meaningful thing that had contributed to each of their lives. He was sitting at the end of a semicircle, and the men on the other side began to describe the people and the events that had contributed significantly to their lives. When each person had spoken, my friend observed the fact that not one single pastor had mentioned the influence of family devotions in his home. He asked the group why no one had included that kind of prayer as a significant event in their childhoods. They all said, almost in one voice, that family devotions for them had been a drag . . . something to avoid . . . something that bored them . . . something that they even hated. And far from making a contribution to to them, family devotions had been something that they remembered with disfavor.

Rev. Dobson, Sr.: I consider our family prayer time to be the most important influence in my life. It wasn't the way it was structured because my mother didn't have any idea of structure. She had no plan and no organization, and she didn't particularly try to make it interesting to us. But she drilled the message into us that she was desperately concerned about our eternal salvation. She got that across to me. She was constantly in prayer about it and so influenced my life that I could weep over it right now in looking back. It wasn't a waste; it was a powerful factor in my childhood.

Dr. Dobson, Jr.: Your mother was a genius at communicating Christianity to children. She died when I was about 10 or 11 years old, but she had a tremendous influence on me. She had a way of making kids feel that this was all there was in life. Didn't she tell you many times that she felt your salvation was the most important thing in her life?

Rev. Dobson, Sr.: She said repeatedly that if one of us was lost, it would be better for her that she had never been born. We knew that she just wasn't saying words. This was a passion with her! And out of that, more than any other influence, came my devotion to God.

Dr. Dobson, Jr.: What is the difference between the impact he felt and what the ministers were describing in the incident I mentioned?

Dr. Wiseman: From Rev. Dobson's experience, it didn't make any difference whether family devotions were interesting or not. It was the passion and concern of his mother that impressed him. Maybe that says something to us.

Mr. Davis: I come from a very similar setting. It was just incredible what my parents were able to do with such a large family. But, man, my dad would read a chapter of the Bible every single day, and every person in the family prayed every single day, from the time we can remember. As a matter of fact, I believe that was the beginning of the reading process in our home for all of us children. We could read the King James Bible before we went to kindergarten because of that habit of reading the Bible around the family altar. There were times that all of us resented it. But the message that came through was that my parents didn't want our circle to be broken in heaven . . . that there were eternal values being communicated to us.

My dad is just getting out of the hospital now, and I asked him at Christmastime, "Dad, how many times have you read the Bible through?" And he said, "I've read the Bible through every year of my life since becoming a Christian, besides studying it in Sunday school." He's a layman who completed only the sixth grade, and he's been a Christian for 50 years. I was surprised by his answer, but he said, "That's nothing. Your mother reads the Bible through twice a year. She's read it through over a hundred times." I'll tell you, you've got to have an idea of what the Word says and have those eternal values firmly in mind when you've studied the Bible like that! My parents were able to communicate that excitement about God's Word and eternal truths to their children.

Mrs. Hull: One of the things that we do to make family devotions interesting for the children is to let them take turns reading. As you said, Jim [Davis], this becomes a big help in learning to read. Then the other thing that we do is urge them to listen carefully so they can ask each other questions about what people were mentioned in the Scriptures. They listen, not only to know the answer, but to try to stump their sibling. Then the youngest child always gets the same easy questions, "Who was Jesus' mother?" And, "Where was He born?" etc. But we found this was one way of making the Bible interesting for them. They are getting older now, and we have devotions on the average of only two or three nights a week because my husband isn't always home.

Dr. Hernandez: I agree with everything that has been said here. In our home, I find that meaningful devotions are also dependent on attitudinal factors, too. If you go into a devotional period when you're rushed or you just want to do it to soothe your conscience, or you choose the inappropriate time to do it . . . maybe the child has just come in from playing and he's tired and fatigued . . . then you're wasting your time. We're human beings and our central nervous system just isn't at our peak efficiency under those conditions. I think you have to use a great deal of judgment and skill and wisdom to select the appropriate moment and appropriate time.

Also, there should be no concretized, absolute formality to the devotional periods. We found if we read one chapter or two chapters every night, it would never work with our children. Sometimes we have to select different approaches. Sometimes in 2 minutes we can get across more to our children than in 20 minutes at other times.

And my attitude is very important. If I come home, like Jim [Dobson, Jr.] has said, exhausted from a day at work in my office, and my wife asks me to sit down and have devotions after supper, that would be the worst time for me to do it. But if I wait 30 or 45 minutes and go upstairs and shower and relax, I am much more ready to handle the situation with my boys. I think there are many variables involved in meaningful devotions . . . how to do it, and how to make it valuable to the entire family.

Dr. Cunningham: You take advantage of the teachable moments.

Dr. Hernandez: That's right.

Dr. Dobson, Jr.: Let me make two suggestions. First, we have an obligation with small children to keep devotions short. If there is a consistent mistake made with preschool children, it's in holding long, drawn-out sessions with youngsters whose attention spans last only 5 or 10 minutes. We sometimes make restless little children hate to pray by keeping them on their knees for a protracted adult prayer about subjects they don't understand.

Second, I take the sixth chapter of Deuteronomy as my guide, where we are commanded not merely to pray with our children, but to talk about God when we get up in the morning, when we go out for a walk; we are to write His Word on our foreheads and on the doorposts of our houses, so that our children grow up in an atmosphere dominated by Christian teaching. This is what my parents and my grandmother did for me. Their Christianity was not kept in one place apart from life. I remember standing in our backyard one day and a plane flew over. My grandmother said, "We need to pray for the men in that plane up there. There is a pilot up there . . . a man who is loved by God." Do you see what I mean? Not all teaching takes place in a bedtime prayer or a period of devotion. It should be part of our casual experience throughout each day.

Mr. Davis: Kids have a way of knowing what their parents really care about. I went through some real difficulty a while back . . . one of those times when I was "down" spiritually. I knew I was not reading the Bible like I should, not praying like I should. I began to discipline myself to fast and to pray, and I was getting up early in the morning, before the children woke up at 6:00 or 6:30, and I was kneeling in the living room by myself praying and weeping before the Lord over some real issues in our lives and in the work of the church and its finances. I didn't hear anyone enter the room, but Debbie had gotten up and saw me praying. She came into that room and crawled underneath my chair and began to pray with her daddy. It was so meaningful because, when she sees me praying, she wants to pray too. God rewarded my discipline by giving me a priceless moment with my little daughter.

Rev. Dobson, Sr.: It's hard to believe, but Jim, here, was praying before he could speak. He saw us pray, and would just get on his knees and mumble, making sounds to God. And I believe he was actually in touch with God, even though he was just a toddler.

Dr. Dobson, Jr.: You know of all the passions in my life . . . the things that I really care about . . . the one that touches me most deeply deals with the salvation of my own children. I think most teen-agers come to a point probably during late adolescence where they stand at a crossroads . . . where one path leads away from everything they've been taught, and the other leads in the direction of a Christian commitment. And they're not able to make this choice objectively, apart from society. There are all kinds of pressures pushing them in the wrong direction.

If I have a request of God that exceeds all other desires . . . including prayers for health and profession and loved ones . . . the most significant thing I want from Him is that He will be there to tip the scales in that moment of decision. I want His divine influence in that moment of choice. I feel as my grandmother did that to lose my children would be the greatest of tragedies in my life, but I'm confident that God is going to hear my prayers.

Dr. Hernandez: I was just thinking as your dad [Rev. Dobson] expressed the sincerity of his own mother and your grandmother. Children can pick up the discrepancy between what we tell them in our devotions and what we really believe. It doesn't matter how much time we spend on our knees and in our devotions if we are not living what we are telling our children. I believe this is one of the primary causes of rebellion in teen-agers. They know when we're phonies. If we're going to commit ourselves, let's do it 100 percent, and that means living and speaking the Christian life until we reflect exactly what we're verbalizing.

Dr. Wiseman: I have a little problem with the matter of absolute consistency. I think I have come to believe that it doesn't exist. I have a kid of 15 and he has seen my flaws. I haven't been absolutely consistent at home; I just am not. Sometimes I'm 90 percent; sometimes I'm 80 percent, and sometimes probably lower than that.

Rev. Dobson, Sr.: Sometimes teen-agers will point to your inadequacies, though, as a weapon. In moods of agitation, they will profess not to believe in you be-

cause they know that will hurt you worse than anything they can do.

Dr. Dobson, Jr.: I have seen that happen.

Mr. Davis: Neil, if you only get down to 80 percent,
then you're doing super. Sometimes I'm minus 10
percent.

Dr. Wiseman: I was trying to find out if it was okay
to say that.

Mr. Davis: But I'll tell you what . . . God uses our
failures too. During the times when I've been a poor
example, the Spirit of the Lord comes to me and says,
"You were unfair and you were unchristian. You had
no right to berate your wife in front of your children."
He convicts me, and sometimes I'm man enough to
apologize to my wife and to my children. Those times
are tremendously redemptive. I think a family needs
to see parents humble themselves when they're wrong.

Dr. Hernandez: I'm certainly no model of perfection
in my home. For any of us here to say that we have
not had any indiscretions in our Christian life would
be to make fools of ourselves. We obviously falter and
fail at some point. But I tell you that every time that
I have . . . when it's obvious to me I have made a
mistake . . . I have gone to my little boys, ages six and
seven, and said, "Daddy made a mistake; Daddy didn't
act the way he should have." And that little boy will
look up to me and he will say, "You're forgiven,
Daddy." He realizes that I'm not perfect, but we are
trying to make amends for our mistakes. Like Jim
said, the Lord uses those times.

Dr. Dobson, Jr.: I had to apologize to my daughter not
long ago. I had been grouchy and irritable with her,
and my conscience wouldn't let me forget it. The next
morning, I told her that daddies are not perfect and
that I had to ask her to forgive me for pushing her too

hard. Then she really stung me. Danae looked up at me with sparkling eyes and said, "I knew you were going to say that, Daddy!"

Rev. Dobson, Sr.: She had you second-guessed from the beginning.

Dr. Dobson, Jr.: I've learned never to underestimate kids!

Dr. Cunningham: But wasn't Dave talking about a consistency of *commitment?* In other words, when there is an obvious lie being lived out in that home . . . when the life-style of that house does not measure up to what is being projected to the outside world. Sometimes members of my staff repeat the wild things that teen-agers reveal about their home lives. I say, "Hey, buddy, be cool with what these kids tell you. Someday your kid is going to be telling some pastor what goes on at your house, and hopefully that minister will be as generous as I want you to be." But on that same point, there are homes where the parents are living an outright lie. When that happens, it sure can produce cynical adolescents.

Dr. Dobson, Jr.: I would like to return to what we were talking about before and give the strongest possible emphasis to the matter of intercessory prayer during the formative years of child rearing. The job of parenthood is too complex for anybody to do perfectly. God will hear that kind of prayer and I believe that He will answer it. I had spoken on the subject of fatherhood at my own church this last November, and I mentioned the fact that from the time our children were very young, Shirley and I have fasted and prayed approximately one day a week for their spiritual welfare. A week after I spoke I received a letter from a woman who had been at the service. She later gave

me permission to publish what she wrote me. Let me
share it with you.

Dear Dr. Dobson:

I awoke at 2 a.m. on Monday, following your message of Sunday, November 2, your words pricking and
invading my consciousness. The burden for my children,
now grown, was overwhelming.

Of course you couldn't speak to fathers without
speaking to mothers also. We cry in the night saying,
"Is it too late to pray for our children?"

They are 25 and 21 years old now. They do not
believe, do not attend any kind of church, reject our
prayers, and do not listen. My son is an agnostic, a
believer in the science of evolution and the philosopher
Krishnamurti. My beautiful, 21-year-old daughter is
deeply involved in Bahai. She does not believe that
Christ is the Son of God. In her own words: "I will
never believe in Christianity."

Today I am nearly 59 years old. In the quiet of the
morning, my mind was retracing the life of our family.
Yes, we were deeply involved in the church. The children were dedicated to God at First Baptist in Ingle-
wood. They were always in the nursery, Sunday school,
Jet Cadets, even to the watchnight services.

Christina accepted the Lord in an evangelistic meeting at Calvary Baptist, Gardena, when she was 9 or
10 years old. Her own decision. But now she tells me
there is nothing to this "myth" of asking Jesus to come
into your heart. She tells me now that she cried and
prayed at night (this little girl) and that Jesus never
came into her heart.

You hit home. There was no guarantee that our
children would really have a valid relationship with
Christ Jesus just because we took them to church and
they were involved in the life of the church. And the
tears start to fall when I admit that their father and I
did not pray for them . . . or with them, for that matter
(except in a very superficial way . . . and when they
got really sick . . . you know what I mean).

Say it again. Parents of little children, intercede for
them now! Woo them and win them to Christ at the

family altar. The church is no substitute for the precepts established in the home.

Thank God for the priorities my old-fashioned, godly parents established in our home. We *knew* when we were out of line, there would be a few swats of the razor strap on our hindsides; and we *knew* that following the evening meal, Papa would read from the Bible. We would all be on our knees around that table as Papa prayed. I can see myself now at age eight, weeping at my chair while Papa prayed. God . . . the Holy Spirit, ever dealing with me at that early age.

We need to encourage Christian laymen like yourself who are using their talents for the Lord.

Don't stop. Say it again and again.

There are some things you can say for parents whose children are not living the Christian life, in spite of what training we failed to give in their formative years.

Commit them.

It is not too late to claim them.

Line up all the promises and lean hard on them.

There are so many other ways in which the Lord can use us to win them . . . yet.

Thank you again for your message. You are part of the family at First Church, and you are loved and prayed for.

Sincerely,

Rev. Dobson, Sr.: That's a powerful letter. I wish every young parent could have that perspective on the salvation of their children. *Nothing* exceeds it in importance.

Dr. Cunningham: It reminds me of one of our retired general superintendents who knew he was near death. Things were winding down and his daughter was with him. They were in his study which was filled with memorabilia, souvenirs, and gifts from all over the world where he had served the church with great dignity and distinguished service. And she said to him, "Daddy, it must give you tremendous satisfaction to sit here and look around this room and see all the accomplishments of your ministry."

He said, "Honey, it's true. These things are very meaningful." But he added, "I've discovered that when you get to where I am, the things that mean more to you than anything else in the world are your children. Nothing else means as much as your kids." Fortunately for him, he had kept his priorities in the proper order through the years, but it is so sad when a person discovers in old age that he was chasing rainbows.

Dr. Dobson, Jr.: My dad beautifully described this spiritual responsibility as being like a three-man relay race. It begins with your earthly father running his lap around the track carrying the baton . . . which is the gospel of Jesus Christ. After he has raced the prescribed distance, the time comes for him to transfer the baton . . . the gospel . . . to you. It then becomes your turn to take a lap around the track. Finally, you must pass that priceless baton on to your children. But as any track coach will tell you, the critical moment in a relay race occurs in the transfer of the baton from one runner to the next. That is the point of greatest danger. That is when the prize may be dropped. That is where races are won or lost.

Speaking as a father, my most important function in life is to get that gospel safely into the hands of my children. Nothing else even approaches that task in significance to me. You see, if my boy and girl don't carry the baton with them, it doesn't matter how fast they run or whether they are first to cross the finish line. Without the gospel, all is lost. That is where my priorities begin, and I'm trying to remember this mission every day of my life.

Mr. Davis: The analogy of a track event can be taken a step further, can't it? I mean, many years of training are usually necessary before the race can be run properly.

Dr. Dobson, Jr.: Yes, the early years of childhood are vital to the eventual outcome during young adulthood. In fact, I have come to believe that the fifth year of a child's life can be the most significant 12 months in his spiritual existence. Until that time, he believes in Jesus in much the same way that he accepts Santa Claus. But sometime between the fifth and seventh years, he either "takes hold" and begins to develop a genuine faith, or he does not. I see that period of time as extremely delicate in Christian teaching. Our best Sunday school teachers should be handling that age-group.

Teaching Male and Female Roles to Children

Mr. Davis: I would like to hear what each of you think about teaching sex roles to children . . . encouraging boys to be boys and girls to be girls. There has been some controversy over this in the last few years, and I would like the group to discuss it.

Rev. Dobson, Sr.: I read a book recently which dealt extensively with that subject. It was called *Sexual Suicide.* The author, George Gilder, feels strongly about the importance of well-defined sex roles because the lines of demarcation have become so hazy. He thinks boys should be taught to do masculine things . . . play football, go fishing, or play the trumpet. They should not be given dolls or tea sets or toys that are traditionally feminine. His opinion is controversial as you said, Jim, but I'm inclined to agree with him. It seems to me that the "identity crisis" we've heard so much about can only be worsened by people not even knowing which sex they represent.

Dr. Dobson, Jr.: Aarlie, do you teach your girls to sew and cook?

Mrs. Hull: Yes. In fact, my eight-year-old daughter is handling the meals for our family while I'm away on this trip. I called my husband last night, and he told me that Heather served beans and franks for dinner. He said there were too many beans and too few franks, but she did pretty well with the meal. She found an item in a cookbook called "ants on a log," which is celery filled with peanut butter and raisins. Then she served ice cream for dessert. It wasn't the kind of meal I would fix, but she's getting some important experience in being a mother.

Dr. Dobson, Jr.: Let me take it a step further. Would you make your boy wash dishes or vacuum the floor?

Mrs. Hull: I might on occasion. I don't see it as any big deal. My husband and son once cooked a meal to surprise the girls and me.

Rev. Dobson, Sr.: Some of these matters are purely cultural, with no real bearing on anything.

Dr. Cunningham: From a psychological point of view, Jim, what is wrong with a little boy having some interest in feminine things, such as dolls, during a certain period in his life?

Dr. Dobson, Jr.: I think it would be a mistake for us to give parents the impression that they have to make super males out of their boys and frilly little females out of their girls. Some moms and dads get all sweaty-palmed when their daughters go through a tomboy period or their sons want to push a baby buggy for a month or two. Their anxieties are usually unfounded. Their great fear, of course, is that the child will grow up to be a homosexual. But just because a youngster leans toward the opposite sex for a while does not mean he will be a sexual deviate later in life.

However, I must admit that I worry about the boy who doesn't seem to know he's a boy and the girl who doesn't recognize her feminine nature. As my dad said a few minutes ago, this problem is related to the "identity crisis" which affects so many young people. When a child doesn't know who he is, what his strengths and weaknesses are, or what his values represent, he is in a very vulnerable position emotionally. And the worst confusion of all is not knowing whether you are masculine or feminine.

Mrs. Hull: Do you attempt to teach different sex roles to your son and daughter?

Dr. Dobson, Jr.: Yes, I do. I relate differently to my son than to my daughter. I try to treat them with equal love and respect, of course, but our sex roles play a part in the relationships. Ryan identifies his maleness with my masculinity. For example, if the family is going to ride in the car, he will say, "Us guys will ride in the front seat and the girls will ride in back." Danae plays the same game with her mother.

Dr. Cunningham: How do you feel about fathers touching their daughters in an affectionate way, and mothers being physical in their expression of love for their sons?

Dr. Dobson, Jr.: Our aversion to incest has made people a little reluctant to be physical with their children. But again, the anxieties are usually unwarranted. My little girl and I have been very physical with each other from the time she was born until now. When she was two or three years of age, I'd watch a televised game on a Saturday afternoon with Danae sitting on my lap for two hours or more. I never realized how important that physical contact was to her until she was in the second grade and came down with the chicken pox. I had never had the chicken pox, and believe me, I didn't *want* the chicken pox. So I avoided her like the plague during that time. I would head in the other direction when she came toward me. This went on for five or six days without me realizing that I was communicating something negative to her. Finally, she went to Shirley in tears. She said, "Daddy won't touch me anymore." She was sensitive to the fact that I was not expressing my love physically as I had before. I think we deprive children of much-needed warmth and love when we are afraid to put our arms around them or pick them up or caress them.

Dr. Cunningham: Well, this concern over homosexuality relates to fathers and sons, too. The literature substantiates the fact that a boy needs to be touched by his dad . . . needs to have affectionate communication with him, even as he does with his mother.

Dr. Dobson, Jr.: Yes, that is true. Physical contact is needed between a father and son, and this, of course, does not cause homosexuality. It usually grows out of extremely unhappy home situations . . . where the child has been given an emotional reason to reject his appropriate sex role. Perhaps his mother showed an aversion for him as a male or the father figure was missing or the mother completely dominated him. There are many possible causes. But I think the most common cause is through massive feelings of inferiority and inadequacy which lead a youngster to hate (and thus reject) himself.

Rev. Dobson, Sr.: But don't we have many homosexuals now who have chosen that way of life more or less deliberately? They have no psychological "excuse."

Dr. Dobson, Jr.: That's right. It's important to understand that sexual energy can be rechanneled fairly easily during an ambivalent period in early adolescence. That's why homosexuality is a "contagious" disorder. It is not always a matter of faulty development. It is pretty well documented that one of the ways homosexuality can get started is for male roommates to catch each other masturbating and then to make a group experience out of it.

Rev. Dobson, Sr.: Is it true that once the sexual energy gets reoriented, it is almost irreversible?

Dr. Hernandez: It depends on how fulfilling the perversion is. If it really fulfills a psychological and emotional need for an individual, then it can be very difficult to treat.

Rev. Dobson, Sr.: Is homosexuality a satisfying way of life for many people?

Dr. Hernandez: Some of the most unhappy people I've known are homosexuals and lesbians, no matter what you hear to the contrary from the media.

Dr. Dobson, Jr.: The position of the American Institute of Family Relations is that homosexuality can be treated successfully, provided two conditions exist: First, the patient must care enough to make a sincere commitment to his own therapy. The "cure" is not something that can be done *to* a person; it's something he has to participate in himself. Second, the therapist must believe that the treatment is worthwhile. More and more frequently, now, homosexuality is being defined as just another normal pattern. The American Psychiatric Association, I believe, declared homosexuality no longer in the category of emotional disorder.

Rev. Dobson, Sr.: Here we need to examine the Word of God. Have you ever wondered why the Bible takes such an absolute, hard line against homosexuality? You couldn't find more severe language than is used in the first chapter of Romans. It doesn't suggest any compromise with homosexuality at all and links this perversion together with the worst sins, including murder.

Mr. Davis: It associates homosexuality with idolatry and giving up the very image of God.

Rev. Dobson, Sr.: It's in the same pot with every evil that you can name.

Mr. Davis: That's right.

Dr. Dobson, Jr.: I think the problem that pastors face is in distinguishing between willful homosexuality, where the person chooses that way of life in defiance of God, as opposed to those individuals who have been twisted and warped and distorted from childhood, almost beyond their ability to cope with and control it.

Rev. Dobson, Sr.: You're saying the person who has kleptomania may not be as guilty as one who steals to get an object?

Dr. Dobson, Jr.: Perhaps so. Let me give an example. I dealt with a high school student who was then 16 years old. He was sent to me by the vice-principal because the boy would not take showers with the other students after physical education. That was a tip-off to me. I confronted him rather openly about his problem. He looked at me and smiled and said, "You know what my problem is?" and I said, "Yeah, I think I do." Then he told me some of his background. When he was 10 years old, his mother and father came home drunk from a New Year's Eve party. He couldn't remember all the details but told me that his father made him "sleep" with his mother in a very disgusting way. He was so repelled by that horrible night that he rejected women completely.

In a case like that, you have a youngster who was forced into something repugnant at a very critical time in his development. Consequently, it has made normal sexual attitudes very repulsive to him. If I were a pastor dealing with this lad, I would have to take a much more compassionate approach than with someone who said, "You know, I thought it over, and I tried homosexual activity and I figured, Why not?"

Dr. Cunningham: Here again, the importance of healthy family life is emphasized. When husbands and wives function within the family unit as designed, then their children are usually blessed with healthy minds and bodies that respond the way God intended.

Sex Education

Rev. Dobson, Sr.: Jim, I believe you are absolutely opposed to sex education courses in schools, aren't you?

Dr. Dobson, Jr.: No. I have been strongly opposed to sex education courses *as they are usually taught* in public schools. The typical program attempts to teach the technology of sex without discussing the morality of sex. In my opinion, these components should never be separated. When you teach physiology and facts without ethical consideration, it's like showing a kid how to shoot a pistol without telling where to aim it. I think a well-designed sex education program in a school could make a valuable contribution, but it would have to incorporate more than the "how to." This is the reason I feel so strongly that the church should provide an instructional program for its junior high and high school students.

Mr. Davis: I agree with the need for good programs in the church, but there aren't enough qualified teachers in most congregations. Anyway, I believe the job of teaching kids should be done primarily by the parents.

Dr. Wiseman: Do you think most mothers and fathers are qualified to do the job properly?

Mr. Davis: Probably not, but at least that's where the *responsibility* begins. Maybe our effort in the church should be concentrated on programs that are geared for *parents*.

Dr. Wiseman: I think we have to be realistic. The church has the ability to produce a good sex education program, but it is in a tough spot. There are too many emotional factors involved. I don't believe it's going to accomplish much just to tell pastors they ought to have these courses.

Mrs. Hull: We're putting our heads in the sand! This is not a topic that we can ignore or table. I wish each of you could have been with my husband and me when we spoke on the subject of sex to students at a Christian college last year. These were nice kids from good Christian homes, but they were grossly misinformed and uninformed on sexual matters.

When we talked about factual information, so many said, "Why haven't we heard this sort of thing before?" It was not just girls that seemed appreciative, but the guys, also.

And when we discussed issues related to morality . . . about God's design for sex in marriage . . . we had maybe 30 notes pushed under our door, saying, "I know what you say is true, but I've already been involved sexually. Now what do I do?"

So Larry and I asked repeatedly, "Why haven't these young people been given some of this healthy information earlier, so at least some of them could have been better prepared to withstand the social pressures?"

Dr. Dobson, Jr.: I agree with you, Aarlie. Young people today are being bombarded with sexual messages that contradict what we believe and what the Bible teaches. They hear it on television, radio, and, most importantly, from other students. But who is presenting the other side . . . the Christian viewpoint? If the church and Christian people remain silent and paralyzed on the issues of sex and morality, then we are not giving our kids a fair chance to choose God's plan.

Rev. Dobson, Sr.: What are you proposing?

Dr. Dobson, Jr.: That the denomination prepare a well-designed package of tapes and printed material for use in local churches. I'm sure Neil is right in saying that this idea won't be received enthusiastically, but it's worth campaigning for. Our kids are at stake.

There's another aspect of adolescent sexuality that we should discuss, if we have the courage. I'm referring to the subject of masturbation, which *many* Christian young people struggle with today. Research on this subject is very clear: Between 95 and 99 percent of boys masturbate, and something over 50 percent of the girls do. I personally believe that the figures are not much different for Christian young people either, although they are often overwhelmed with guilt for it.

Dr. Wiseman: I would guess that upwards of 70 percent of male students in a Christian college who struggle with spiritual conflicts are actually facing this problem.

Dr. Dobson, Jr.: That is why I raised the issue here. Some of the most frustrated Christians I've counseled have been young men who simply could not suppress the urge to masturbate. I think it's important to remember that the sex drive in males is stronger at 16 years of age than at any other time of life, and some fellows find it *impossible* to control their impulses. Then the act gradually becomes a major spiritual issue, and a young man really begins to suffer. And I mean *suffer!*

He promises God that he will never do it again, and

begs His forgiveness. Then he manages to abstain for a week or two, or even five or six. But sooner or later, the inevitable happens. Hormonal pressures become more and more intense until he dreams about sex at night and thinks about it in the daytime. He fights it 24 hours a day, but then in a moment of weakness, his resistance crumbles, and he does the very thing he solemnly promised God he would not do. When his passion finally cools, he has to face the Almighty again with fear and trembling. And what does one say when he has broken his 200th promise to God? I'm convinced that a certain percentage of the young adults who go through this trauma eventually give up their faith to escape the unbearable guilt.

Mr. Davis: In your view, is masturbation sinful for an adolescent?

Rev. Dobson, Sr.: The Bible is absolutely silent on this subject from cover to cover, which ought to give us some indication of how God views it. I don't think He would leave out instruction along this line if there was a deadly sin to be avoided.

Dr. Cunningham: Here is how I counsel men about it. (I have never had the question raised from a woman.) I feel it is possible to give this needed physiological relief without necessarily "fantasizing" and concentrating on lustful thoughts. This is an important point. While the Bible is silent about the masturbatory act, it is not silent about lust. And Jesus, of course, said if you commit a forbidden act in your mind, you have sinned nonetheless. So I don't think it is acceptable to obtain this release in a lustful way . . . perhaps, say, with a *Playboy* magazine. I think if a sincere, committed Christian can recognize the physiological dynamics of this, knowing why the urge is developing within him, and can get a release from the tension

71

without lusting, then he can maintain a victorious spiritual life.

Mr. Davis: There are obviously many different opinions among Christians on this subject.

Dr. Cunningham: I always precede my comments on this subject with words very similar to yours . . . that we have no final conclusion based on the Word of God, and that good and committed people feel very differently about this emotional topic. Ultimately, each individual has to resolve it in his own way.

Dr. Dobson, Jr.: It is my understanding that Bill Gothard categorically condemns masturbation as sinful in all cases.

Rev. Dobson, Sr.: I believe that is the greatest mistake that a teacher or preacher can make. It can destroy a sensitive adolescent . . . emotionally and spiritually.

Mr. Davis: David Wilkerson takes the same position. He distributes pamphlets which condemn it as sin.

Rev. Dobson, Sr.: He must have some justification from Scripture; what does he give? The Bible is our final Resource.

Dr. Cunningham: Let me say again that I am absolutely opposed to promiscuous masturbation. I mean looking forward to it, planning it, cultivating it as part of an ongoing sex life. I'm talking here about the severe pressure that builds up simply because of the physical dynamics involved.

Mrs. Hull: Jim [Dobson, Jr.], what do you recommend that Christian parents tell their children about this subject?

Dr. Dobson, Jr.: I approach it very cautiously, trying not to offend those sincere Christians who have drawn conclusions that differ from my own. After all, they may be right and I may be wrong. I tell them, quite frankly, that I can't say with absolute confidence what God thinks about the act of masturbation. I can only share with them what I *believe* He wants of us: It simply does not seem reasonable to me that God would put a raging fire in an immature adolescent, offer him few if any biblical guidelines, but then damn him eternally for doing something he cannot prevent. I agree with Paul [Cunningham], however, that this is not a free ticket for a boy or girl to let their minds feast on lustful thoughts and ungodly literature.

Mrs. Hull: Specifically, what should a parent say to a pre-teen-age boy?

Dr. Dobson, Jr.: Let me quote you what my dad said to me when I was 11 years old. We were taking a long trip in a car when this important subject came up. He said, "I'm not telling you to do this. In fact, I hope it never becomes a problem for you. But if it happens, I don't want you to go through what I experienced. I've prayed about it and searched the Bible, and I've come to the conclusion that it probably doesn't have much to do with your spiritual life." That one statement spared me much of the guilt and anguish that some of my Christian friends endured in the years ahead.

Dr. Wiseman: I think this ought to be included in the book which comes from these discussions.

Mrs. Hull: Can we go back to Paul's concept of fantasizing? Since I'm not a man, I'll have to ask: Is it really possible to release the physical pressure without fantasizing?

Dr. Dobson, Jr.: Again, nothing is going to keep some young men from thinking about a physical relationship with a woman. None of the traditional approaches work, such as cold showers or plenty of exercise or light bed clothing. What we have to recognize is the existence of an irrepressible hormonal system that was designed to guarantee the continuation of the human race. God created that urge, and it is as inevitable as the appetite for food and water.

Dr. Cunningham: I'm talking about self-discipline here. I'm talking about a total Christian experience. This is keeping your body under subjection, just like you're going to have to eventually learn to do in all aspects of your thought life. The whole discipleship syndrome is one of learning self-control. I think this should be a part of that entire concept.

Rev. Dobson, Sr.: That's a good point, Paul. But I would like Jim [Dobson, Jr.] to comment on the curious psychological phenomena that seems to be at work here: If you try to force sex completely out of your mind, it can work in reverse. It's like trying to fight a fire with gasoline.

Dr. Dobson, Jr.: That is a well-understood principle. "Forbidden fruit" is always more attractive than that which is easily available to us. For example, I can resist donuts and chocolate cake pretty well until I go on a rigid diet. But once I know that sweets are "untouchable," I crave them every day. This human characteristic is particularly relevant to sexual interests. Promiscuous adolescents who "sleep" with many partners often become bored (or even disgusted) with sex. By contrast, the teen-agers I have known who felt guilty over every sexual impulse have been those most obsessed with masturbation and lustful thoughts. If my understanding of these psychological forces is correct, the best way to keep a child from becoming compulsively addicted to the act of self-gratification is to minimize its importance in his life.

Rev. Dobson, Sr.: Then where does self-control fit in? We all know that the discipline Paul referred to is a scriptural truth.

Dr. Dobson, Jr.: It certainly is and the concept should be taught to teen-agers; but as Paul implied, it is a *learned* response that may occur little by little. What is possible for a 30- or 40-year-old man may not be possible for those youngsters in the passion of adolescence.

Maybe I am rationalizing, but I see it this way: You don't expect a three-year-old to exemplify the personality of Jesus in every detail. You don't expect him to be giving and loving and be able to "turn the other cheek." (There are many Christian adults who don't "turn the other cheek" very well, either!) In other words, toddlers are in a developmental phase where they don't correspond to many of the characteristics of mature, adult Christianity. And I perceive the period of early adolescence in a similar way. It is a developmental phase wherein sex is new and terribly exciting and, for males, never very far from conscious thought. They will probably calm down somewhat in the years ahead, but during their late teens, they don't conform to the highest ideals which Jesus taught. That should come with greater maturity and self-discipline.

Dave, we haven't heard from you. What are your views?

Dr. Hernandez: Well, I don't run into the same counseling problems that you do, Jim, but I agree that this is something that we are not going to be able to stop. We shouldn't heap unresolvable guilt on youngsters who are masturbating. What I am afraid of is that we will create an environment where we encourage it. This thing perpetuates in married life and then it becomes pathogenic. Then you have serious difficulties. We also have to remember that a man and wife were created to fulfill each others' needs, and that's the way it ought to be. The unmarried adolescent doesn't have that avenue of release, however. The heart of the issue has to do with the meaning of "lust" as Jesus defined it.

Rev. Dobson, Sr.: Again, the Scripture is our ultimate Guide. I quote James 1:14 and 15: "But every man is tempted when he is drawn away of his own lust and enticed. Then when lust hath conceived, it bringeth forth sin: and sin, when it is finished, bringeth forth death."

Let's look at a specific situation and see if it will clarify this scripture. Since sexual desire is a natural appetite, it helps my understanding to use one of the other appetites—the desire for food—as an illustration. Thus: If I'm ravenously hungry and walk past an apple stand, the very sight of the delicious red apple sets my mouth to watering. But because I have no money, there there is no way I can *lawfully* gratify my desires. No one is watching. "Steal it," Satan suggests. That suggestion of sinful behavior is what I believe James means by the term "lust." It is temptation to gratify a legal desire in an *illegal way. But temptation is not sin.* Jesus was tempted three times in the wildnerness, but He remained sinless. Therefore, "lust" as used in this sense *is not sin.*

Dr. Dobson, Jr.: Then the fellow standing at the apple stand is still completely innocent, even though he has thought about stealing the fruit?

Rev. Dobson, Sr.: Until and unless his *will* says, "I'll steal if the opportunity presents itself," the man is innocent before God. The moment he says in his heart, "I will," sin enters, whether the opportunity ever presents itself or not.

The late Dr. R. T. Williams, in his book *Temptation, a Neglected Theme,* helped me tremendously at this point. He said something like this: Think of illegal desire (or lust) as the male and the *will* as the female. *There can be no sin until the desire to gratify in the wrong way unites with the will;* at that point sin is conceived.

Dr. Dobson, Jr.: In other words, if a man is walking down the street and is confronted by a girl in a miniskirt who has deliberately dressed in a provocative manner, he remains innocent even though she "scores a hit" on his sensory apparatus.

Rev. Dobson, Sr.: That's right. Temptation is the devil knocking at the door, but temptation is not sin. Sin occurs when you unlock the door and invite him in.

Dr. Dobson, Jr.: Without that understanding of the difference between temptation and sin, a Christian can be flogged to death by unnecessary feelings of guilt. He is fighting to suppress a biochemical mechanism which God himself created.

Rev. Dobson, Sr.: Someone said, "Quit apologizing for sex. You didn't invent it." Unfortunately, however, sex has such an aura of guilt about it that Christians have difficulty even discussing the subject without being blinded and confused.

Dr. Dobson, Jr.: There is one clarification I would like to add to the definition you gave. It is possible for the will to yield to temptations other than outright sexual relationships. In other words, Satan may tempt us to dwell on unclean thoughts . . . to play and replay them through the mind . . . to fantasize and corrupt the thought life, as Paul has said. This can become a willful act too, can't it?

Rev. Dobson, Sr.: Of course it can, and Jesus commanded us to control our thought life as we read in Matt. 5:28.

Dr. Hernandez: Returning to our earlier topic, what if

a youngster desired a particular girl and went home and continued to fantasize about that same girl as he masturbated?

Mr. Davis: What if? What is the verdict then?

Rev. Dobson, Sr.: I think that is what he must not do.

Dr. Cunningham: Jesus spoke rather clearly to that point. The Bible says this kind of fantasizing is tantamount to adultery, even if no overt act occurs.

Dr. Dobson, Jr.: To me, the concept of lust involves much more than simple desire. It could be represented by my saying to a woman, either verbally or attitudinally, "I don't care what I do to you or what our sexual union does to your body; I don't care about the children who may be conceived from this act or the diseases we may exchange; I don't care what our irresponsibility does to your future relationship to your husband or within your present marriage; I don't care about you as a person, and I'm unconcerned about what this act is going to do to your eternal soul or how it will be viewed in the eyes of God. I *will have my way* with your body, regardless!"

You see, if that is my attitude, it doesn't matter whether I get around to the sex act or not . . . I have committed adultery in my heart. That attitude is unquestionably sinful. And I think that's what Jesus was condemning. It's very different from the spontaneous electrical charge that a man gets when an attractive woman walks by. And the man who can suppress that charge totally is either too old to care or he's a young man in considerable trouble. God created that electrochemical energy.

Mr. Davis: That is a well thought out statement, Jim [Dobson, Jr.]. I could not have expressed myself like you have, and this has really helped me today. I see the great danger of a "will" that compromises with lust . . . where the person plans ways and opportunities to be promiscuous . . . where he is willing to establish an illicit relationship at the expense of his family or his relationship with God. When I stop and consider the majesty and holiness of God, in no way do I want to displease Him in my thought life. That stops the whole process of lust for me completely. Yet I've had to work this out with God through a process of growth. I think it's going to be difficult to get those kinds of concepts on paper for the benefit of our readers.

Dr. Cunningham: Dave, what about physiological needs in women?

Dr. Hernandez: Females have essentially the same kind of needs, although they have been able to sublimate them because of cultural pressures that have been placed upon them. Women do have a greater capacity for postponing gratification than men. For instance, if a married man goes away on a business trip for two or three weeks, he will probably be much more edgy than his wife who has been waiting for the same time. She's much better prepared to handle long periods of deprivation.

Mrs. Hull: That's interesting. I've always wondered about that. What conclusions can we draw from this discussion?

Dr. Dobson, Jr.: Let me summarize my views on the subject of masturbation with as few words as possible (even though we all may not agree at this point). There are three circumstances in which this act is dangerous and damaging: First, when masturbation occurs in a group setting, the implications are entirely different than when it is a private event. Secondly, masturbation in marriage replaces the expression of love and intimacy which God intended for a husband and wife. (And surprisingly, I've found that it is extremely common among married adults of both sexes. Studies put the figure at 30 percent or greater.) Thirdly, masturbation has the potential for destroying a healthy personality by creating unresolvable guilt. It is in this third area that I have the greatest concerns.

Regardless of whether Christian parents view this act as sinful or not, I feel they should talk to their children during the preadolescent period and tell them how to cope with the experience, when (and if) it occurs. As for God's views on the subject, I believe every Christian must work that out for himself. I only know what I think He has communicated to me.

I would like to say to our readers that we recognize the delicate and controversial nature of this topic, and that there will undoubtedly be conscientious Christians who will disagree with our conclusions. Certainly, the "safest" approach would be to edit these comments from our book. However, we feel an obligation to help the many young Christians who struggle desperately with the moral issues associated with masturbation, and have elected to include the entire discussion. We can only ask for tolerance and understanding as we seek the will of God in this important matter.

NOTE: Dr. James Dobson has recorded a set of tapes on which he talks directly to pre-teen-agers about the experiences which will soon engulf them. The album, "Preparing for Adolescence," contains six tapes devoted to the subjects of low self-esteem, peer group pressure, sexual development, and the meaning of love. The final tape presents a rap session with four teen-agers who explain their own adolescent experiences. This album can be obtained in Christian bookstores or can be ordered from Box 952, Temple City, Calif. 91780. It can be used effectively by parents and pre-teens together, or by larger groups in a church setting.

Television

Dr. Wiseman: We can hardly talk about family life and the training of children today without focusing our attention on television and its impact on our homes.

Rev. Dobson, Sr.: I personally feel television is the most destructive element in our society today.

Dr. Dobson, Jr.: I strongly agree. Shirley and I watched a program a few nights ago which typifies the direction TV is going. It made me want to throw my shoe through the screen.

The name of the weekly program is "One Day at a Time," and it is one of those many shows which tries to deal with a different "untouchable" subject each week. The setting for the series is focused on a woman who has been divorced after 18 years of marriage. She has two teen-age daughters and they live in the same apartment building as the mother's current boyfriend. During this particular program, the boyfriend, David, told the divorcee, Ann, that he had to go out of town on a weekend business trip.

While he was gone, Ann needed to get into his apartment for some reason, and requested that the building superintendent use his master key to open David's door. No sooner had Ann stepped into David's living room than a giggling young woman came running out of the bedroom, with David in hot pursuit. She was dressed only in pajama tops, and David was wearing the other half of the set. There was a moment of shock and disbelief as all three participants gasped and glared at each other. Then to my amazement, the audience broke into a spontaneous applause. I'm still not sure for whom the ovation was intended or what message it conveyed, but it was followed by an adolescent titter from the audience . . . the kind of giggling that occurs among kids when something is not really funny . . . just racy. Ann turned in a huff and stalked out of David's apartment, slamming the door behind her.

The rest of the program was devoted to helping Ann see how wrong she was in getting upset over David's escapade. "All men fool around," she was told. He was only doing what is natural. Ann's two teen-age daughters were especially supportive of poor, misunderstood David and his swinging girl friend. Finally convinced, Ann called David on the telephone and apologized for *her* misconduct; and in the final scene, she is shown going out of her door on the way to David's apartment, ostensibly to give him what he was getting from his other playmate.

You see, the thing that irritates me about these programs is that they are not merely reflecting society . . . they are shaping and changing it! In this case, David's deceit ("I'm going out of town") and his pajama game were presented as noble behaviors. Ann and her outmoded morality were resoundingly condemned.

Dr. Cunningham: Was that a soap opera?

Dr. Dobson, Jr.: No. "One Day at a Time" is listed as a comedy in the *TV Guide*. Some comedy!

Mr. Davis: This is one reason we don't have a television set in our home. Another reason is what it does to your interaction with other family members. Because we don't have TV to watch, we look to other activities for entertainment which are much more creative; and as a result, there's less boredom in our lives now. In my opinion, TV causes tremendous boredom. We have so much entertainment and sports and interests to occupy our minds that people just seem to be saturated with it all; and I wonder if that doesn't have a lot to do with the violence we are experiencing in our society. People are looking for new sources of stimulation . . . even if it involves rape and murder.

Dr. Wiseman: Jim [Davis], how did you reach the decision to get rid of your television set?

Mr. Davis: Well, a friendly burglar made the decision for us. Someone broke into our home and rescued us from some of our materialism. We bought another set but sold it when we moved to Bend, Ore., and just never replaced it. There are disadvantages to not having this contact with the world around us; but we've been without television for four years, and Beverly and I have never regretted our decision.

Dr. Wiseman: How did you explain it to your little girl?

Mr. Davis: Debbie is five years old and all the kids in the neighborhood do have television. Occasionally she says to me, "Daddy, why don't we have a television set?" and I sit down and try to talk to her about it. Basically, the programs she likes best on TV are the cartoons; but the last time that I watched cartoons, I was disturbed by their violence and by the commercials which sponsored them. I mean it sincerely. So I try to explain my feelings to Debbie. It doesn't change her mind that she would still like to have a television, but at least I find her doing other things, such as reading and drawing and riding her bike. She could ride a bike at four years of age, and she loves hiking and running. Her physical skills have improved in almost every area. I'm not saying what we've done is for everyone, but we feel good about it for ourselves.

Dr. Dobson, Jr.: I admire your discipline in that area.

Mr. Davis: So much of the programming has no place in our home. The April, 1976, issue of *Reader's Digest* carried an article titled "Sex and Drama in the Afternoon," and it said 67 million people watch soap operas every day. Devotion to those programs is apparently sweeping the nation, even among college and university students. And the point of the article was that people are *identifying* with the characters, who are involved in illicit sex, abortions, homosexuality, and every form of personal intrigue. One lady wrote and demanded that the writers let a certain pair of lovers get married. She had rented a wedding dress four times in order to get "married" along with them in a mock ceremony before the television set.

Dr. Wiseman: We have a little lady in my home church who sometimes requests prayers for the people on the soap opera. That's not a joke.

Mr. Davis: Come on, Neil!

Dr. Wiseman: I'm serious. This little lady is a widow, and she lives alone. She fantasizes every day that she is one of the characters in the drama.

Dr. Dobson, Jr.: The reason television attracts . . . the reason people enjoy watching it . . . is because of identification. If you did not identify, you wouldn't really enjoy the programs as much. This makes television doubly influential. For example, it stands to reason that if the average child "participates" in 18,000 murders during his 14 years of life, his attitude toward violence and bloodletting *has* to be affected.

Mrs. Hull: "Helter Skelter" was on television a while back, which told the story of Charles Manson and his "family" as they brutally slaughtered so many people. One girl in my church asked me if I saw it, and I said, "No." She said, "It just made me sick at first, but then I got used to it."

Dr. Dobson, Jr.: That program drew a tremendous audience, nationally . . . greater, in fact, than any other program that year. I can't understand its appeal. Why would anyone want to see a screaming, pregnant woman being stabbed repeatedly in the abdomen? That is a mystery to me. What satisfaction could there be in watching the peaceful, middle-aged LaBianca couple being cut to pieces? Public interest in those kinds of bloody pictures says more about the American people than it does about television itself. We have a strange concept of "entertainment."

Dr. Hernandez: We have developed an insatiable appetite for blood and gore. My concern is that we are becoming desensitized to many things that we ought to be repelled by. I got into a heated discussion about this with one of my colleagues at USC, where Jim [Dobson, Jr.], and I serve on the faculty. I had been invited to one of the sexual dysfunction seminars in which they planned to show a series of hardcore pornographic films to the physicians, nurses, and paramedical staff in order to *desensitize* us. One of my colleagues, whom I hold in high esteem, wanted to make me feel bad because I wouldn't participate.

"Well, Dave," he said, "one of the most prominent sexual dysfunction counselors in the United States had to undergo this desensitization process in order for him to fulfill himself and in order to be of value to anybody else." To accomplish this, he stood nude in front of the mirror and began to scream perverted obscenities at himself. My friend said, "If you want to get desensitized, that may be what you'll have to go through."

And I said, "Well, if you fellows want to make fools of yourselves standing nude in front of your mirrors, then go ahead, but I know what is in good taste and what is not in good taste. Besides, I have as satisfactory results in my practice as you guys do without being desensitized." I think we are getting to a state of desensitization where *nothing* repels us, no matter how evil or awful or ridiculous it is. Television has played a key role in this process.

Mr. Davis: That's another way of saying that the conscience is being stifled, isn't it? Our responsiveness to right and wrong has been deadened.

Dr. Hernandez: That's right. And I am also concerned about the inaccessibility of parents who plant their preschool children in front of a television set hour after hour. TV offers a convenient way to get rid of kids through most of each day.

Dr. Dobson, Jr.: A major study was conducted recently at Harvard University in which the researchers concluded that the most important period of a child's intellectual life occurs between 18 and 36 months of age. A large part of his future academic ability and mental agility seem to depend on the verbal interaction and intellectual stimulation of that early period of life. If that is accurate, and I believe it is, then we have reason to be concerned about youngsters watching countless hours of "mindless" television a week. (One poll shows that the average preschool child watches 54 hours of television each week.) During those critical formative years, a major portion of his time is spent in a hypnotic trance before the "flickering blue parent."

Mrs. Hull: That problem of parent inaccessibility was also reported in the *Christian Medical Journal* recently. It stressed the damaging ways television interferes with conversation and interaction between parents and children.

Rev. Dobson, Sr.: Along another line, I am concerned about the close relationship between the movie industry and television. The kind of motion pictures being produced today are more destructive and evil than ever before, yet in a few years they will appear on television for our children to see.

Dr. Dobson, Jr.: I've noticed that even magazine and newspaper reviewers are complaining about the filth and disgusting scenes that are shown routinely in movies today.

Rev. Dobson, Sr.: Sure, the rotten stuff being produced is repulsive to every decent citizen, not just the Christian community. But what I find hard to understand is why we have become so self-conscious about fighting this vile trash. Our own denomination took a lonely stand against the movie industry more than 50 years ago. Our early leaders saw that it was destined to deteriorate and increasingly appeal to lust and greed. Now that their concern has been vindicated for all to see, we have largely abandoned the battle. We fought through the heat of the day, but now that our disgust is shared even by independent reviewers, we somehow seem to feel that it is old-fashioned to condemn the movie theater. Let me say, speaking for myself, that I am unalterably opposed to an industry which thrives on illicit sex, profane language, glamorization of the pleasure principle, and every form of filth.

Dr. Cunningham: And as you said, that trash isn't

confined to the theater; it is already evident on our TV sets as well.

Dr. Dobson, Jr.: We seem to be in agreement that television has a harmful impact on meaningful family life. But what should be done about it? In a way, we are like the mice who agreed that there should be a bell on the neck of the cat, but no one seemed to know how to get it there. Do any of you have some specific suggestions? How can we "bell the cat"?

Rev. Dobson, Sr.: We can no more hope to reform TV than we can reasonably expect the early conversion of the devil himself. I believe that it is true because television combines the availability of vast fortunes with the lust of the general population. That's an unbeatable combination. The question is, Do the few scraps of "food" mixed with so garbage justify the tube being in our living room or not?

Dr. Wiseman: I think it is unrealistic to ask people to get rid of their television sets.

Mr. Davis: I agree that most people would not accept that recommendation. But facing the fact that TV is here to stay, how can it be controlled in our homes?

Rev. Dobson, Sr.: I have a quote from *International Intercessors*, June, 1976, commenting on a recent article in *Newsweek* magazine:

> In a recent *Newsweek* article, "The Quiet Hour," Robert Mayer appeals for 60 to 90 minutes of TV silence in the early evening when the American family might have a chance to dine quietly together and be free from the noisy bombardment of TV commercials and entertainment. He points out that family members are becoming strangers to each other and need some special time to "get to know" one another and share common interests. Mr. Mayer wistfully admits that he does not expect advertisers and TV stations to consider his suggestions favorably, but, nonetheless, points out many advantages in such a "blacking out" period.

Mrs. Hull: That is an excellent idea. My fear has been that television would dominate our homelife or be a central part of our children's experiences. I had been praying about that problem when our set broke. (Maybe those events were connected!) It took us four months to get the set fixed, and in that time we sort of "broke the habit." We made a point during that period to play games with the children, read to them, and get involved personally with them. That really changed our family life. Our 10-year-old has read every one of C. S. Lewis' "Chronicles of Narnia," as well as his science-fiction trilogy. It opened the whole world to him, and today he'd rather have books than television.

Dr. Dobson, Jr.: Aarlie, I feel obligated to ask you a very practical question on behalf of our readers. I doubt if there are very many solid, committed Christians who would not agree that what you have done is a healthy and admirable thing. But where did you get the energy at the end of each day to interact with your kids in that way? Most of the people I know have nothing left to give by nightfall, particularly since relating to a small child requires a certain kind of energy that is in short supply in most homes by the time dinner is over.

Mrs. Hull: All right. That is true, but you see, my children are older now—10, 8, and 6. And the scrubbing of my floors has a low priority for me.

Dr. Dobson, Jr.: You save something for your kids.
Mrs. Hull: Yes.

Dr. Cunningham: It often comes down to priorities, then, doesn't it?

Mrs. Hull: When my husband was in a medical residency, we were very limited in all of our finances. I was forced to evaluate my own priorities. My husband is a very meticulous person. He likes to have everything in perfect order, and he really got on me about this. He motivated me to be very careful about the maintenance of the house. Then like you said, at the end of the day, I found myself having done nothing but cleaning and sort of trying to keep the kids out of the major problems.

Then I heard someone say it is constructive to visualize your funeral and think about the things you want people to remember as they sit looking at your coffin. It's a morbid thought, but it influenced me. And I sat one day and visualized my funeral and I thought about the things that I wanted my children to recall about me. I couldn't get too excited about them saying, "Mother really kept a beautiful, clean house," or my husband saying, "She was real careful about hanging my white shirts beside by blue ones." Is that all they will remember? No! I have to admit that my house was demoted on my list of priorites after that, but I was happier in my role as wife and mother.

Dr. Hernandez: That's beautifully said, Aarlie. But let me ask you this: How did your husband react to this decision?

Mrs. Hull: I shared my views with him. We sat down and we talked about it, and I bared my soul. He understood me and could relate to what I felt. As a result, we were both able to compromise. It wasn't a conflict.

Dr. Dobson, Jr.: Is your television set still broken?

Mrs. Hull: No, we have three shows the kids can watch. They can watch "Little House on the Prairie," "The Waltons," and one other. I just can't tell you how much nicer it has been not to have television be such an important aspect in our lives. And now the kids don't even ask about it. They don't even say, "Can we watch such and such?"

Dr. Dobson, Jr.: Paul, what responsibility does the church have with regard to television?

Dr. Cunningham: I think the church has a heavy responsibility in teaching its people. First, the thrust is to greatly reduce the amount of television viewing done by the entire family, and second, to carefully screen whatever your children are viewing. Christian ministers ought to be reminding their congregations that television is not without danger and potential harm. It must be controlled or it will control *us*.

Dr. Dobson, Jr.: Another suggestion which I've found helpful is to watch certain programs *with* my children. Then the activity becomes something we're doing together instead of doing it in isolation. Night before last, there was a Charlie Brown cartoon on television which I watched with my kids. We all three loved it. It became a "togetherness thing," which is very different from plopping a child in front of the set and walking off.

Mrs. Hull: It's more fun for the kids if you're there.

Dr. Dobson, Jr.: Yes, it's always more fun to share a pleasure with someone you love.

Rev. Dobson, Sr.: Before we leave the subject of television, I would like to comment on its potential for good. There is a broad movement now within the conservative Christian community for personal evangelism. I'm certainly not opposed to that concept, but we shouldn't ignore the opportunities fo mass evangelism, as well. Now a man can step to a microphone and speak to perhaps 60 million people at one time! What a vast resource this is for both good *and* evil. Jim [Dobson, Jr.], you reached more than 5 million people a day when you were on the Dinah Shore television show, which is more than you will speak to personally in a lifetime.

Dr. Wiseman: When I sat next to Pastor Paul Moore, awaiting the start of his telethon to raise money for his Lamb's Club church in Manhattan, I realized for the first time that one man was talking about his project to several million viewers. It was overwhelming to me to think about how effective mass communication methods are today.

Dr. Dobson, Jr.: To summarize this discussion of television, then, I think we should admit that we have no magic answers that will save us from its impact on our families. Like so many other areas of difficulty in our lives, the solutions involve self-discipline and determination. We *can* control television if we choose to do so, and I suppose the thrust of our comments has been to warn parents of the dangers of letting TV dominate our homes.

Pastors and the "P.K.'s"*

Dr. Dobson, Jr.: We've agreed strongly that mothers of small children should reserve some prime time for their families, but I feel we should go a step beyond. I'm equally concerned about the amount of time which fathers spend with their small children . . . particularly pastors and ministers.

Dr. Cunningham: That is one of the greatest burdens that I bring to this setting today. I've been in the ministry long enough to know that we pastors often need help more than any other people in the church, not because we are "bad" fathers or "bad" husbands, but because the very nature of our jobs calls for us to be all things to all people . . . to be everything to everybody. And we go to bed at night with guilt because of what we haven't done, even though we may have worked 18 or 20 hours to do what we did. Then our attention is turned to our own children who may not have seen us for two or three days. The pressures on pastors can be enormous.

---

*Preachers' kids.

Dr. Dobson, Jr.: This is why I raised the issue, Paul. As I travel back and forth across the country to speak, I find pastors caught in an inevitable trap. It is impossible for them to accomplish everything expected by their congregations, so they feel guilty for taking any leisure time away from the church. However, the failure to be with their families creates great guilt of another sort. So they lose on both counts and face constant pressure from all sides.

Mrs. Hull: What is the solution?

Dr. Dobson, Jr.: I have been recommending that pastors hit the issue head-on from the pulpit. Instead of "sneaking away" to be with his family on Monday, a minister should denounce the tendency of American males to abandon their responsibilities as husbands and fathers in favor of incessant work. I would like to hear a minister say, boldly, "I am going to set an example which I hope will be imitated by every male member of this congregation. I will be taking one day a week specifically to be with my wife and children. It will be very difficult to reach me on that day, because it is designated as a time of rest and recreation within our family unit. I don't apologize for this decision; in fact, I am doing what I believe we must *all* do if we are going to hold our families together in these stressful days. 'Go thou and do likewise'!"

Mr. Davis: That's a workable concept, Jim, which I believe must be supported by those of who are laymen in the church. If there is anything that I tried to do for my former pastor, it was to get him to relax, to spend some time with his family. He carried such a heavy responsibility that it was difficult for him to take his kids fishing or just spend quiet times with them. He was so busy counseling and building a church and

94

preaching and pastoring that he had nothing left to give at home.

Dr. Dobson, Jr.: No one can do it all.

Mr. Davis: It's impossible! I think we would have more of a New Testament Church if we could educate the laymen to be supportive of their pastors in the preservation of their homelives. Instead, we interrupt his dinner hour . . . we call him to get other members' telephone numbers . . . and we expect him to attend church functions six nights a week.

Mrs. Hull: Also, pastors sometimes have a false impression of what it is their parishioners really admire in them. Speaking as a layman, I think we admire ministers who have strong families even more than we do those with other virtues and abilities.

Mr. Davis: Neil, you mentioned that some pastors' wives have to work just to keep their husbands in the ministry. That would make sense to me if congregations were in poverty, but most churches are not that poor. I don't understand how a church could let a fellow struggle and sweat in order to serve their spiritual needs. It was a great shock for me to learn that a former pastor of mine earned less than I did as a schoolteacher, even though he led a church with 1,000 or more members.

Dr. Dobson, Jr.: You know what I find more intolerable? My dad, here, has been in the ministry for 40 years, and he will be eligible for retirement next year. I learned recently that his pension will offer a staggering $73.00 a month! Forty years' service has produced $73.00 a month. He's not going to starve to death for other reasons, but what if he had to exist on that amount? I think our laymen need to be educated on this matter. They should demand that the financial needs of their pastors be met, not only during their youth, but in old age, too.

Dr. Cunningham: The retirement program for ministers is a lot better now than it was a few years ago, thank the Lord.

Dr. Wiseman: Getting back to the pastor's day off, which day should he take? We've talked about Monday being his family day, but the kids are in school then.

Dr. Dobson, Jr.: I was with Paul Bersche, Missionary Alliance pastor in Detroit, recently, and he has faced that same question. He said that Monday is not a day for a pastor to spend with his family for the reasons you mentioned. He has designated Saturday as their family day, even though he has to preach on Sunday. He just makes sure his sermons are prepared by Friday night. He said any other day of the week could be restful for him, but it is not a day of family togetherness unless the kids are out of school.

Rev. Dobson, Sr.: The important thing is for pastors to keep their families high on the list of priorities, and not be totally "married" to their work. We've all seen some tragic outcomes when pastors' kids grow up as "church orphans."

Mrs. Hull: But what about circumstances which can't be avoided? I know people whom I respect very much who have had to sacrifice their family life. I had a friend whose husband took a mission assignment, and as part of that responsibility, the children were going to have to go to boarding school. I knew this girl very well, and I asked her, "How can you say 'good-bye' to your children like that? That would tear me up. I don't think I could do it."

She said (and I've heard the same thought from others), "The Lord wants us to do this, and I'm trusting the children to Him." I want to ask you gentlemen, Do you think the Lord wants those kids out of their homes during these impressionable years?

Rev. Dobson, Sr.: I faced this problem in the evangelistic field when Jim [Jr.] was just a little guy. It's real! It's heart tearing, but I approached it this way: I felt I had to do what God called me to do, so I had no choice but to leave. However, I established a home and left Jim's mother with him. I would then be home every two or three weeks, and during holidays. We were, of course, together all summer too. It was difficult for my wife and me to be apart, but we did it to maintain the stability of our home. I believe this is essential.

Dr. Dobson, Jr.: I will always appreciate that sacrifice made for me, because I know what it cost you. But as Aarlie said, others are facing this same decision today. I received a letter two days ago from a missionary in Ethiopia who asked me for advice on that same issue. She and her husband just arrived on the field, and they were going to have to make a decision as to whether to keep their kids with them or send them to a boarding school. She asked how I felt about it and I wrote them back yesterday. I said if the child were mine, I definitely would keep him with me at all costs. The educational and academic aspect of his training is not as important as what I would want to transmit in values and attitudes and spiritual development. I really feel it is wrong to disband the family unit if there is any other alternative.

Mrs. Hull: It is simplistic to say, "Trust the Lord to take care of the children."

Dr. Dobson, Jr.: There is a kind of misunderstanding among Christians which says, "If you do the work of the Lord with all your might, God will save your children." That is not true. I wish it were. Many people seem to believe that, but it isn't supported by Scripture. There are numerous examples of godly men, such as Samuel, who lost their own children.

Dr. Cunningham: I am married to a missionary's daughter who at the age of five and a half, was sent to boarding school in Africa, where she saw her parents only about three times a year. This represents the most severe kind of sacrifice that a missionary has to face. I have had the privilege of ministering to the children of missionaries, and I think it can be safely said, and I want to say this very carefully, that those children who have had this experience often never fully recover from it.

My wife, for example, was "put down" when she was in the school because of the strong anti-American sentiment there. She was the only American in her school. We're not talking about a child 10 or 12 years old, but only 6. All in all, it has made her a tremendously strong person; she is a unique and marvelous person, and I doubt if she would have been all that she is to me and to our children had she not had those tough experiences. But at the same time, were she not from strong English stock with tremendous gifts and graces, I don't know . . . maybe she would not have survived, because others haven't.

I can't feel that it is a good policy at this point to make this the only answer for these families . . . to separate tender little children from their parents. I know of one situation, for example, where the children have to take a long ride in a riverboat to see their parents; I'm talking about *little* children. It's a trip of several hours to their mission compound. Their mother says good-bye to them in the fall, and she does not see them for many months because of the expense involved in travelling. They could be taken by helicopter instead of the riverboat ride, but they don't have the money. We must do something to assist people like this, whatever the cost.

Summary comments at the end
of the first day's discussion

Dr. Dobson, Jr.: Can I ask for a bit of outright honesty on the part of the people around this circle? Has anybody else been convicted today, besides me, to do a better job of practicing what we preach? I don't know if anyone has been going through what I've been experiencing, but I want to do a better job tomorrow as husband and father than I did yesterday. Am I the only one?

Dr. Wiseman: We feel the same way. The Holy Spirit has spoken to me through these issues.

Mrs. Hull: But that should be conveyed to our readers, too. We all see our inadequacies and failings.

Dr. Wiseman: None of us ever operates at optimum efficiency. Some days it's pretty bad.

Dr. Dobson, Jr.: As a matter of fact, we should face the problem of guilt in parenthood. No matter what you do, it is impossible to avoid some regrets and shortcomings.

Dr. Wiseman: I just spent an evening with some friends in Denver who have two boys in college. One of them is a sophomore and the other is a freshman. The kids came home the other day and began criticizing their parents and saying what they wish had been different in their home. They came from a strong Christian family, but they made their parents feel guilty and depressed. I said to the father, "What

99

would your feelings have been if you had been an alcoholic?" He said he wouldn't have felt any more guilty than he does now. There is a difference between deserved guilt and the guilt that comes from wishing you had done a more perfect job. Some of us need to free ourselves from wishing we had done everything exactly right. That is a destructive kind of guilt.

Mrs. Hull: Of course, the question is, Do we ever do the best we can? I don't. I could do a better job of raising my kids now than I did when they were small. I recently took care of some children whose father had leukemia for three months, and, wow, was I a good mother to those kids! Why couldn't I have had my children at this point in my life?

Dr. Wiseman: Yeah, I was a better pastor at 35 than I was at 22.

Mrs. Hull: And that's part of our guilt . . . because we look back from where we are now.

Dr. Dobson, Jr.: Even if you did your absolute best, it still wouldn't be sufficient, because kids are infinitely complex little creatures. Besides, society squeezes us into its mold and pressurizes us and leaves us exhausted.

Mr. Davis: Which brings us to the need for God's leadership and guidance. Parents should admit their inadequacies to the Lord, and present the problems to Him in prayer and fasting.

Dr. Hernandez: I agree very strongly, Jim [Davis]. This is not a book of chastisements. When we see how badly we fail, we are made aware of our dependence on God. All you have to do is read the newspapers to become despondent.

Just to give you a little description of what I mean, there's a physician at USC who has written a top-notch book on the subject of gynecology. This past year his life has practically disintegrated before our very eyes. He has an only son . . . a brilliant fellow . . . who graduated from high school this year and is going to Harvard. Suddenly it dawned on the father that he was like a complete stranger to his son. He has worked himself into a frenzy these past six months trying to catch up . . . trying to bring about a meaningful relationship with his son. Now, the boy is leaving home and his dad realizes he has failed as a father. He has turned to alcohol. His wife is about to divorce him. And he has almost gone berserk. He's had to seek out psychologic help, and, in fact, he's on the verge of lithium therapy, long term, for manic depression. The despair of finding himself unable to capture what he has lost is almost beyond his ability to withstand.

So this is not something that just happens within the church. It is happening out there in the secular world, too. We just have to throw ourselves on the mercy of the Lord and tell Him that we have failed again, and we're going to pick it up from there. So this shouldn't be a book of chastisement, causing our readers to throw their arms up in despair. It must be a book of hope!

Dr. Dobson, Jr.: And our hope is rooted in our faith!

The Abortion Issue

Mr. Davis: Dave, are you getting more requests to perform abortions now than a year or two ago?

Dr. Hernandez: You have no idea how much pressure is on us as physicians. Women are *demanding* abortions . . . not for medical reasons, but as "retroactive birth control" measures. They come in and insist that this procedure be done.

Mr. Davis: What answer do you give them?

Dr. Hernandez: It depends on their reasons. I will perform an abortion for a woman who is a victim of incest or rape, or where there are severe medical problems. It's not a pleasurable experience to terminate a pregnancy like that, but it sometimes has to be done. But I see many women who are absolutely irresponsible . . . those who were simply careless, not just once, but repeatedly. I've had some patients who have had three or four abortions done by other physicians.

I had a patient in my office the other day who was 21 years old, but she had a cervix that looked like that of a 45-year-old woman. This girl is not married and I said, "Young lady, when did you begin having intercourse?"

She told me, "I started having intercourse at age 13."

I said, "How many partners have you had since then?"

Then she thought for a while and said, "I don't know how many partners I've had. I don't think I could even count them."

I said to her, "Are you happy? Are you being satisfied? Is this what you want?"

And at that point she got very, very solemn and tears started flowing down her cheeks. She said, "No, to be honest with you I am disliking it more and more."

Then I turned to her and said, "What are you really looking for?" I had a meaningful opportunity to witness to her. But I see so many sad cases like that.

Mrs. Hull: Did you have a medical reason for asking her when she first became sexually active?

Dr. Hernandez: Yes. We now have scientific proof that the earlier a young lady starts having intercourse, the more frequently she experiences it, the more babies she produces, and the more partners she has, the greater will be the risk of cervical cancer. This is now a proven fact. So if I see a young lady like this, I put a red star on her chart . . . not to label her an immoral patient, because I don't moralize on my charts. Rather, to alert me to the possibility of cancer of the cervix when she is age 40 or 45.

Mr. Davis: Did you say giving birth to many babies increases the risk, too?

Dr. Hernandez: Yes. But let's look at the opposite extreme. What happens in the case of women who have never been pregnant, such as nuns. A woman who has had no sexual exposure has a *much* lower rate of cervical cancer; in fact, the disease is almost unheard of for this group. However, she will have a higher incidence of cancer of the endometrium (the lining of the uterus). Now, what does that tell us? I believe it says that the Lord has a plan for our lives. First, a woman should get married at an appropriately mature age. Second, she should have sexual relationships with one man . . . her husband. And third, she should have a sensible number of children.

Dr. Dobson, Jr.: That's a beautiful observation.

Dr. Hernandez: God has demanded moral behavior from us for *our* benefit. And if we choose to disobey this commandment, we will pay for it!

Dr. Wiseman: Do you think people have illegitimate children in order to get more welfare money?

Mrs. Hull: I've seen some evidence of that.

Dr. Wiseman: It's a pretty tough way to get a few bucks.

Dr. Dobson, Jr.: An uneducated woman with five children can stay at home and do better financially on welfare than she can in the working world.

Mr. Davis: Neil, in the first teaching assignment I had in an elementary school in Monrovia, Calif., a mother came into the office with seven children. Every one of the kids had a different father. When she filled out the enrollment forms, she was asked, "What is your occupation?"

She said, "Prostitute, and the best one in Monrovia."

The principal and the secretary of the school (both were women) said, "You can't write that down!" And she said, "Why not?" That was in 1961.

Dr. Wiseman: How much money did she get every month to support her seven kids?

Mr. Davis: She certainly had enough money to put beer in the refrigerator and keep men around. I believe there are thousands of other cases like hers!

Dr. Dobson, Jr.: Furthermore, the welfare arrangement is such that it would discourage her from getting married. She would lose her income if she had a working husband.

Mrs. Hull: Another thing that disturbs me is the lack of status that children have been given in recent years. They are just not seen as the blessings from God that they used to be.

Dr. Cunningham: They have become a burden to us, haven't they? It's not uncommon to hear people say, "I'd hate to be raising kids in this day and age."

Dr. Dobson, Jr.: *Esquire* magazine, March, 1974, devoted its cover story to the question, "Do Americans Suddenly Hate Kids?" It explored the many ways American parents reveal that children are a bother. They cost too much money, they keep women from having their own careers, and they are a nuisance to the pleasure-oriented. Perhaps we were too child-oriented during the fifties, but now the pendulum has swung to the other extreme.

Rev. Dobson, Sr.: That attitude tends to cheapen life at every level.

Dr. Dobson, Jr.: I understand a very common scene in divorce courtrooms involves the parents fighting over their children . . . neither the mother nor the father want them and both struggle to avoid the responsibility.

Rev. Dobson, Sr.: Dave, I would like to return to the abortion issue and ask you a personal question. Don't answer it if you think it's not proper; but what is your response to the women who come in wanting abortions for reasons of their own?

Dr. Hernandez: I call my receptionist and I tell her the present appointment will take about 45 more minutes. I ask her to notify my other waiting patients of the delay and suggest that they get a cup of coffee or something. Then I discuss all aspects of the issue with my patient. When I am convinced that she has, in my opinion, made every effort to protect herself and she realizes that this is not a glib decision, I will occasionally perform an abortion. Now, many times I have refused to do it. I take a very serious approach to it; I just don't say, "Okay, I'll call my receptionist and schedule the surgery." I don't do that.

Rev. Dobson, Sr.: Do you take the position that the physician ought to have a prerogative of choice in matters related to abortion?

Dr. Hernandez: Yes. And I'll tell you why. I have difficulty imposing my views even on the physicians within my own practice. We have seven men in our group who are board certified. I never engage in any conflicts with my associates, even though one of them tends to be more liberal. I try to influence them by my life. I don't argue with my patients, either, because moral issues are not resolved by argumentation.

Rev. Dobson, Sr.: Dave, with due respect to you and the thoughtful position you've taken, I would be dishonest if I didn't express my unyielding opposition to abortion for reasons other than the ones you listed (rape, incest, medical problems, etc.). For us to take a healthy, normal child and terminate his little life is contrary to everything I believe. I could not even support a politician who would favor unrestricted abortions. I will never cast a vote that would cause us to lay a hand on an unborn child. To do so would, for me, be a violation of my Christian principles! I feel this very strongly. To kill a child who has a normal expectancy of a full life is to me nothing short of murder.

Mr. Davis: I would tend to agree with you, but there are difficult issues involved. My two brothers work in a ghetto area in Los Angeles, and I talked to them last night. They tell of kids 11 and 12 years old who are having sex on a regular basis, and of course, many of the girls get pregnant while they're still in junior high school! They can't possibly take care of the babies, and there aren't enough adoptive homes for minority kids. It's a difficult problem.

Dr. Hernandez: That has played a role in my attitude, of course. Ten years ago when I was delivering babies at Booth Memorial Hospital, we were having between 80 and 90 deliveries a month of unwed mothers between the ages of 13 and 21. Approximately 95 percent of those babies were being adopted. Now the whole thing has reversed itself. We deliver about 150 babies a month in my group, and I haven't seen one teen-ager allow her baby to be adopted during the past four years!

Dr. Cunningham: My experience is identical with yours, Dave. In the early portion of my ministry, I can recall no unwed pregnant girl wanting to keep her child. But more recently, I have not had one mother who was willing to give up her child.

Rev. Dobson, Sr.: The stigma is gone.

Dr. Cunningham: Recent studies show that 20 percent of American children do not live with both their parents. With this increased number of fatherless children, what kind of morality . . . what kind of structure are we going to have in the days ahead?

Dr. Dobson, Jr.: Let me add another statistic to the one you just quoted, Paul. Half of the brides are pregnant at the altar. Can you imagine the impact of that circumstance on the American family? Fifty percent of all young couples begin their married life with the biological, emotional, and financial stresses of pregnancy. They are not only busy trying to adjust to one another, but they're faced with the pressures associated with parenthood at the same time. It's no wonder so many families don't make it.

Mrs. Hull: Most of those girls couldn't possibly be prepared for the responsibilities of motherhood.

Dr. Hernandez: It's tragic. I will ask 13- and 14-year-old single girls . . . most of whom are on welfare . . . "Have you made preparations for this child? You realize this is a lifetime responsibility . . . not just a nine-month commitment." They will look at me and say, "Oh yes, I made preparations. My mother is going to help take care of the baby." But as soon as that baby is born, he goes on welfare and the vicious cycle is repeated. That same girl will return a year or two later with another pregnancy. I have had some girls who have produced four or five children, all from different partners, all on welfare. This is the problem, of course, that Jim [Davis] has mentioned. These are not babies who are being brought up in good homes. They are already handicapped. Many will be unloved and lonely and miserable. And so this is the problem that confronts us.

Rev. Dobson, Sr.: I know what you say is true. However, some of the greatest men in history have been born out of wedlock, including Leonardo da Vinci. The moral issue can't be settled by taking the position that "they don't have a chance, anyway."

Dr. Dobson, Jr.: It took me several years to evaluate the ethical and moral issues involved in the abortion question, but I am now adamantly opposed to the concept of abortion on demand. I just can't see how God could possibly condone the killing of more than a million unborn babies in America each year.

One of the factors which influenced my viewpoint was the biblical references to God's knowledge of certain individuals *before they were born*. The Book of Luke says that John the Baptist was filled with the Holy Spirit even before his birth! Jesus, of course, was conceived by the Holy Spirit in Mary's womb. And a reference is made in the Book of Genesis to the twins, Jacob and Esau, who fought with each other before they were born. The Lord knew them as individuals and told Rebekah that they would be rivals throughout life and would each father a great nation. The most striking example, however, is a beautiful passage found in Jeremiah 1, verses 4 and 5, where the prophet says, "The Lord said to me, 'I knew you *before you were formed* within your mother's womb; before you were born I sanctified you and appointed you as my spokesman to the world'" (TLB).

To me, these references refute the notion that we human beings do not have a soul or a personhood until we are born at full term. How would God have judged the prenatal destruction of Jeremiah or John or Jesus or Jacob and Esau? I now believe I know the answer to that question.

Rev. Dobson, Sr.: If that reasoning is valid, and I believe it is, then society's hands are stained with the blood of a million infants a year!

Mr. Davis: Jim, when you referred to the "killing of a million babies" a year through abortion, I'm sure you meant to call them babies instead of fetuses, didn't you?

Dr. Dobson, Jr.: Yes. It is interesting to me that a woman who wants her pregnancy always refers to the life inside of her as "my baby." I've never heard a woman talk about "my fetus" unless she had terminated its life.

Dr. Hernandez: I can understand your viewpoint, and I'm not so sure that a strong antiabortion stance isn't the right one. However, I tend to be rather pragmatic in my life, and I try to accept circumstances which I can't change. The abortion movement is with us to stay, and we are unlikely to alter it very much. I certainly don't feel we can correct the matter by legislation, because it is difficult to legislate morality.

Rev. Dobson, Sr.: Dave, it is *already* legislated. The Supreme Court rulings have the impact of law, so this issue is in the hands of attorneys now. Frankly, I don't feel the doctors *or* the attorneys should be saddled with such an important and weighty decision. It should be determined by the people at large.

Mr. Davis: Through a constitutional amendment?

Rev. Dobson, Sr.: Perhaps so.

Dr. Cunningham: Dave, when do you consider a fetus to be viable?

Dr. Hernandez: Well, it has a potential for life outside the uterus at about 20 weeks, although there are exceptions. I've had them survive at 18 weeks. Statistically, a 20-week-old fetus has less than a 2 percent chance of survival. At 25 weeks it has a 10 percent chance of living, and at 30 weeks, the survival rate is 30 percent.

Dr. Wiseman: So when we hear about the 20-week limit for abortions (that's been in all the literature), only 2 percent of those fetuses could live outside the womb?

Dr. Hernandez: Less than 2 percent, actually.

Dr. Cunningham: Are there other ethical dilemmas that you face in your practice, Dave?

Dr. Hernandez: Even tougher issues are right around the corner. Within a year, for example, we're going to hear of infertile couples contributing sperm and egg cells, which will be cultivated in a test tube and reimplanted in the uterus. That is in the immediate future. Is it right to "play" with life in this way?

Dr. Dobson, Jr.: The most troubling moral decision for me concerns aborting a defective or damaged fetus. Amniocenteses are performed rather commonly for older mothers, where a needle is thrust through the abdomen to draw out some of the amniotic fluid which surrounds the fetus. Then by examining the cells under a microscope, a pathologist can tell whether or not a child has Down's Syndrome (mongolism), Tay-Sachs Disease, or other major defects. But what then? Is it right to destroy those defective fetuses?

Dr. Hernandez: We are having to make these difficult decisions every day.

Rev. Dobson, Sr.: I wouldn't want to be in that position.

Dr. Dobson, Jr.: I saw an emotional film at Childrens Hospital recently. It was an actual documentary which showed a newborn child with Down's Syndrome. This little fellow not only had mental retardation and the problems associated with D.S., but he had an intestinal blockage as well. The intestinal problem could have been corrected very easily by surgery, but his parents refused to sign a permission statement. The pediatric surgeon refused to perform the surgery without parental authority, of course, and no court would intervene. It took the baby about 10-12 days to starve to death, but they let him die! The documentary showed his deterioration each day, and the agony of his parents and physician. It was a most distressing film.

Dr. Hernandez: These are very real situations that are happening each day. Let's suppose that that child could have been identified before he was born. Would the parents have been justified in aborting him at 10 to 20 weeks gestation? We have to be very careful what we recommend here, because you can see how devastating it would be to a young couple to be condemned by the church for a decision to prevent such a birth.

Mrs. Hull: I'm sure pastors are being asked for guidance by people who face that kind of difficult question. I wonder where they turn for *their* answers?

Dr. Cunningham: I believe it would be wrong for this group to try to answer such serious questions at this time. Any glib response from us would accomplish very little. I would like to see some sort of official position formulated for the church on abortion, genetic responsibility, the right to life and death, vasectomies, tuboligations, etc. Pastors need some guidelines in these areas, but the questions are too difficult to be answered casually.

Dr. Dobson, Jr.: That's an excellent suggestion. Abortion is, after all, a moral question, and the church is in the business of dealing with such issues.

Rev. Dobson, Sr.: You know, I was thinking the other day about the declining birth rate and the choice of many American women not to have children. Of course, it's an individual woman's right not to become a mother if she wishes. But there's something ambiguous about calling something a "right" when if it were universally practiced, it would mean racial suicide. If every woman drew the same conclusion, it would mean the end of humanity in one generation.

Dr. Dobson, Jr.: The Chinese and Indians don't seem to be contemplating that move.

Rev. Dobson, Sr.: In George Gilder's book *Sexual Suicide,* he said that zero population growth brings with it great national demoralization and despair.

Dr. Dobson, Jr.: Why, because the stability of the older generation depends on having a younger generation around its feet?

Rev. Dobson, Sr.: That's part of it. Our children are the primary tie to the future. When men and women are raising children, they think about saving and building and growing. But, in the absence of children, this creative energy is dissipated on the present.

How the Church Can
Aid the Family

Dr. Dobson, Jr.: We have agreed that one of our primary purposes during the remainder of this day will be to offer some suggestions to pastors and church leaders with regard to how they can help the beleaguered family today. Someone must come to the aid of the institution of marriage and parenthood, and if the church doesn't do it, who will?

With that introduction, then, where do we go from here?

Christian Counseling

Dr. Wiseman: We should offer some advice to pastors who face so many emotional and marital problems in their congregations but have little training for handling them. The least we should do is make some suggestion regarding how to find good referral sources in the community.

Mrs. Hull: Yes, that would be helpful.

Dr. Dobson, Jr.: I would strongly suggest that the pastor have lunch with the professional to whom he is considering referring clients. Ask him what he feels about the principles of the Bible . . . about morality and infidelity and about his general philosophy. A counselor or psychologist who wants those referrals will be glad to give that time. I will not refer to anybody until I've done that.

Mr. Davis: The trouble is, not every town has competent professionals in this field. There is not one common-sense, Christian counselor in Bend, Ore. There are two psychiatrists in the town whose values I question, and another guy out at the junior college. It's incredible! If you have a sexual problem, for example, you are often sent to the University of Oregon in Eugene, to watch films for 16 hours in two days. Effective resources are just not available.

Dr. Dobson, Jr.: I know you're right. Joyce Landorf and I held a family forum in Seattle, Wash., where there were 750 people in attendance. As always, many people asked for counseling from us during the seminar, but time limitations made it impossible to meet the need. Therefore, we got the names of five or six people who were recommended as being competent in that area, and I announced at the end of the Family Forum on Saturday night that we would provide those names. When I began to read them, it looked as if a third of that large crowd grabbed for a piece of paper. I could not believe it! Five years ago, they would have been ashamed to admit their problems. Now, many are seeking help but there are so few qualified therapists.

Mrs. Hull: My husband and I are aware of only two psychiatrists in Seattle whom you would consider to be evangelical Christians.

Rev. Dobson, Sr.: Neil, are you giving the young ministers at your college more courses than heretofore to qualify them along these lines?

Dr. Wiseman: Yes, but I don't think we're doing enough. I think the seminary is doing more now than in the past.

Dr. Cunningham: Of course, the risk here is that if a pastor offers his services as a counselor, he can be overwhelmed by the number of requests. In my own training, I have had more than the average exposure to this kind of material. My goal was never to become an amateur psychiatrist or psychologist. My studies were designed only to provide me with the skills necessary to discern the difference between a spiritual problem and neurosis or psychosis . . . and only to deal with people at that point. I must admit, however, that it is becoming increasingly difficult to find enough competent professionals to whom I can refer.

Dr. Wiseman: I don't believe a counselor has to be an evangelical Christian in order to help someone. It is better if they are of that persuasion, but when a patient is about to have a break with reality, we have to find help for him.

Dr. Cunningham: I don't insist on a Christian in the case of my referrals. I'm looking for competent people. Naturally, I'd prefer that they were evangelicals.

Dr. Dobson, Jr.: I disagree with both of you. A person can be a good gynecologist or a competent dentist and still be an atheist. That is not true in counseling. Eventually all emotional problems relate to values, such as who you're married to, and who you're going to stay married to, and what you believe. Those values and attitudes can't be separated from the personality and emotional structure. So, I'm very careful not to put my stamp of approval on someone whose views are going to run counter to what the patient believes.

Dr. Cunningham: We're talking about two different things. We have a psychiatrist in our community whom I would not consider to be Christian, but he has a very strong value system. He does not take exception to the church in what we believe, but attempts to reinforce what his patients believe. I admit, though, that this professional is probably atypical in this regard. I certainly would not refer to someone who would contradict basic ethics and beliefs.

Mr. Davis: Jim [Dobson, Jr.], what would you suggest for the pastor who can find no acceptable counselor in his community? How can he best help troubled people?

Dr. Dobson, Jr.: There are a couple of suggestions which might be helpful in his approach. The most important contribution he can make is to say, "I love you. I care about you, and I want to hear what you are feeling and what you are experiencing." There is tremendous therapy involved in just listening and in caring and loving. It conforms to the commandment "Bear ye one another's burdens." That loving support is extremely valuable in defusing pent-up emotions and ventilating anxiety. The one universal condition which emotionally distressed people reveal is a need for acceptance and respect. Love is a marvelous "healer" for psychological problems.

The second suggestion is a product of the first: Because you have loved the person and established a certain rapport, you are then in a position to lead him toward more responsible ways of coping with his problems. Perhaps you recognize more alternatives than he does. Whereas alcoholism or drug abuse or extreme anger or running away may be the only approaches that an individual can see to a particular problem, you can perceive other possibilities. Once you have established a love relationship, then you're in a position to say, "Have you thought about this?" or "Would you consider that?" This is where old-fashioned common sense and wisdom are invaluable. If pastors do those two things, they can alleviate many problems, even in the absence of extensive psychological training.

Mrs. Hull: That's good, Jim. That's exactly what we need.

Dr. Cunningham: Usually when a counselee says to a marriage counselor, "You are so understanding," you know what he usually means. He is saying that we have listened with compassion, with concern and interest . . . something any loving husband or wife could have done.

Mr. Davis: Jim, you wrote on our list of proposed topics for today, "Rescue the Family." I'm thinking that the most thorny problem affecting family members today is an absence of that "I love you, I'm interested in you, I care for you." If we can get families to reinstate those messages to each member, they won't be needing outside help.

Dr. Dobson, Jr.: Yes, self-worth is the central core of the personality, and it thrives on old-fashioned love.

Dr. Cunningham: Maybe some of you are acquainted with a systems approach to counseling. I'm just getting into it, but the concept makes sense to me. It involves counseling with the whole family, rather than just one person. The designated patient is only the tip of the iceberg. In other words, strange people and strange behaviors are usually the result of strange families. Unless damaging conditions within the family are corected, then the patient is going to go right back into the same turmoil that caused his original problem. There seems to be some wisdom here for the

118

church. I'm wondering with some of these problems if a pastor may be well advised to have a whole family in his study and give everybody a chance to say what is going on at their house . . . and begin to interrelate some of the problems.

James Fraymore describes it this way: Saturday morning, Dad's in the family room, Mother finds Daughter's room a mess and starts screaming. Dad's ulcer begins to burn as he grabs his golf clubs and leaves. Now Mother is upset. Why does she have to be the policeman and provide disciplinary leadership for the entire family? Meanwhile the daughter is saying, "I've been wronged and I'm very angry at my mother." Whereas all these members of this family are distressed as individuals, each problem is interrelated.

As you mentioned before, Dave, a wife is usually the one who will seek professional help, but the problem is not hers alone. Are you familiar with the "Colorado Study," where one sample of patients was committed to hospitalized psychiatric care, and a comparable sample was placed in stable family homes? Ninety percent of those treated in the homes responded successfully and two years later were doing much better than those treated in the hospital. What this says to me is that we would have fewer emotional problems if our families were stronger, and we can help troubled people most directly by acting to strengthen the relationship between individual family members. And when we counsel, we might do well to get the whole family involved in the situation, instead of one of the more vocal members.

Mr. Davis: That is an important concept. It seems to me that we're witnessing a breakdown in the "chain of command" within the family. But God has linked us all together . . . He has specified how we are to

119

relate to one another. Therefore, a problem with one person will almost always involve his other "team members" as well.

Dr. Dobson, Jr.: I have found it beneficial to talk to individuals first to get them to express what they couldn't say in front of a group. Then when I have accomplished that purpose, I bring the entire family together with the benefit of the information I was given on a one-to-one basis.

Mrs. Hull: One thing that bugs me a little is that we seem to sit around and wait for the denomination or some organization to produce new programs and seminars. I wish local churches would use more initiative to develop their own approaches to family issues. What I'm saying is that I want to see everybody get involved and quit waiting for a new curriculum or program to be laid in our laps.

Mr. Davis: This is, I believe, the ultimate solution to the problem of people who hurt. If people in the church could be taught to lean on each other, support each other, pray for each other, then the pastor would not have to spend so much time counseling. It was said of the early Christian Church, "Behold, how they love one another." I wish that were invariably true today. One of the neat things I love about being around Jim and Shirley and their kids is that they are supportive of how Beverly and I are trying to teach and train our own children. And likewise, I feel we are perhaps being supportive of what they are trying to teach in their own home. We pray for each other and try to contribute any way we can. This is a fantastic cure for isolation and loneliness.

Dr. Dobson, Jr.: At our church, we have developed a concept called "Circles of Concern." Individual Sunday school classes are divided into "circles" of five to eight couples which assume spiritual responsibility for each other. They pray for one another, often meet socially one night a week, and make a point to undergird a weak member or someone in trouble. I can tell you that when the circles function as intended, everyone is strengthened because of it.

Dr. Hernandez: I really think that the Circles of Concern concept has been one of the greatest ideas ever developed in our church. I admit I rarely attend their meetings, primarily because I don't get home until after they begin. But there have been many times when I have gone through a spell where I have been down physically, and it never fails that the next day somebody from the Circle will call and say, "I was just thinking about you, Dave." And it's just amazing what that has done to lift me up. And I just never have ceased to be amazed at what the Lord has done with just one or two phone calls. About a month ago, I was really having troubles, and I got a card from someone who said, "We've just been thinking about you. We want you to know that we love you and we're praying for you and hope everything is fine."

Mrs. Hull: What does it take to send a card?

Dr. Cunningham: Time.

Mrs. Hull: But not much.

Dr. Dobson, Jr.: Over and over again it's been demonstrated to me that people come to a particular church for the first time, not because of its theology, or the building, or the pastor, or the music, or the location. They come to church the first time because they think, Maybe somebody will need me and love me there. They sit in the pew with their hand on their pulse, asking, Am I accepted here? Do I have a place here?

Am I going to have self-esteem here? I firmly believe that many of them walk out the front door never to return because nobody grabs them while they are there. In a Sunday school class I taught, we had 405 people who visited us during a one-year period, even though we were running only about 90 at the time. I believe we could have held many of those who looked us over if the class members had descended on them in love on that first Sunday. You talk about an opportunity to win people to the Lord! I think this is more productive than "banging on doors," or advertising campaigns, or contests, or the other approaches.

Mr. Davis: How do you get a church to be conscious of that opportunity?

Dr. Cunningham: It has to be taught repeatedly from the pulpit and then reinforced by the leading laymen. A program like Circles of Concern is a good place to begin.

The Justice of God

Dr. Dobson, Jr.: I would like to refer back to a comment my dad made about an hour ago, regarding "creative energies being dissipated on the present" (rather than investing them in the future). This relates to my observation that some Christian churches are departing from the "future orientation" which the Bible teaches. Jesus' entire ministry points toward the *future.* Concerning the problems that we face each day, He said: "In this world *ye shall have* tribulation: but be of good cheer; I have overcome the world." He was obviously cautioning His followers to remember that our hope lies not in *this* life but in the next.

Now, what does that have to do with family relationships? Absolutely everything, in my view. We Christians are much better equipped to withstand the trials and sorrows of this existence if we have our eyes focused on the promise of a wonderful life to come. And just as importantly, we are stronger in resisting temptation and evils if we are conscious of an eventual day of judgment and punishment being prepared for the wicked. Do you follow what I am saying?

Rev. Dobson, Sr.: Certainly, and it represents a concern that has literally been burning with me lately. Not only is the emphasis being placed on the present rather than the eternal, but the justice of God seems to have become an outmoded theme. We're being taught a distorted concept of God's nature; He is characterized not only by infinite love but also infinite justice.

Dr. Cunningham: A pendulum never stays in the same place, and perhaps for too long a time most of the preaching emphasis was on the threat of punishment without the balancing message of God's love. Now it has swung to the opposite extreme. I hope there can be a blend between these two essential elements.

Dr. Wiseman: The Word of God teaches both truths.

Dr. Dobson, Jr.: And both truths are important in holding families together! For example, an awareness of God's justice helps husbands and wives remain faithful to each other, and to spend their money wisely, and to take good care of their children, and to make wise choices. It is important for them to know they will someday be held accountable for each day's behavior. That understanding encourages Christian responsibility!

Rev. Dobson, Sr.: Do you counsel with Christian couples who don't seem to recognize their accountability to God?

Dr. Dobson, Jr.: Yes, and this is what brought me to introduce this topic. I am seeing too many married couples who profess to be Christians, but have fallen into the trap of infidelity. In one brief period, I counseled 19 families who had either been unfaithful, or else an extramarital affair was seriously threatened. All 19 of these families were members of the same adult Sunday school class. But that is not an indictment of a particular class or group. Their behavior is common in other churches, too. And what concerns me is that many such couples have not been told that they will one day stand before the judgment bar of God, and their lives will be laid bare before Him. I can tell you that as a teen-ager, this concept of accountability kept me on the "straight and narrow."

Mrs. Hull: It has to be one of the shocks of my life to realize that infidelity has crept into the church.

Dr. Dobson, Jr.: The permissiveness of the sexual revolution does not stop at the front door of the church. Sitting in our pews on Sunday are people who are deeply involved in sin of all varieties. And we'd better not forget that we Christians are also products of our society, and still vulnerable to the deceipt of Satan.

Rev. Dobson, Sr.: If it's in the church, then there is a definite place for the warning note in the ministry. This has been one of the theme songs of my ministry. But I feel we are neglecting the greatest dual motive for obeying God: desire for heaven and fear of hell! Preaching these combined truths has twice the impact, but ministers seem afraid to present both scriptural truths. We used to hear of the consequences of evil in revival services, but revivals are becoming less common, too. We have bought a bill of goods on this, being overly cautious not to hurt our image or drive away some people whom we might otherwise win.

Mrs. Hull: I agree with Rev. Dobson. There is a place in the ministry for the justice of God. I believe in the authority of Scripture. William Barclay expressed it so pointedly. He said it is foolish to use a known consequence of evil as a justification for not participating in it. To do so tends to imply that if you avoid the consequences, then it's no longer sinful. But if Jesus condemned something, it remains sinful, regardless!

Rev. Dobson, Sr.: I think a pastor should present all the major themes of the Bible in each year. There are really not many, and most are catalogued in the sixth chapter of Hebrews. The subjects that are listed there are called the "principles of the doctrine of Christ," and include (1) "the foundation of repentance from dead works"; (2) "faith toward God"; (3) "the doctrine of baptisms" (that is, water baptism and the baptism with the Holy Spirit); (4) "resurrection of the dead"; (5) "eternal judgment"; and, of course, (6) the doctrine of "perfection" (Heb. 6:1-2). It is reasonable that the preaching agenda during the course of a year should include all those themes. If not, why not?

Dr. Dobson, Jr.: I would like to challenge every pastor and every Sunday school teacher who reads this book to look over that list of themes. If any items are skipped, an explanation is in order. That explanation should not come to us but to God. If the Bible stresses a subject, and if the inspired writers considered it worthy for inclusion in God's Word, then by what authority do we take it out? We inconspicuously edit the gospel, not by contradicting it or cutting out sections with a pair of scissors, but by simply ignoring the less popular themes!

Mr. Davis: I read the other day that "silence is not always golden, sometimes it's just yellow."

Rev. Dobson, Sr.: The things you don't say speak with

a loud voice at times. One of the best ways for a pastor to suppress unwanted truth is to simply keep quiet about it and also to select carefully the men who fill the pulpit when he's away.

Dr. Wiseman: We not only have the problem of the things left unsaid, but I would like to see ministers be accountable for their messages. It would be healthy for our pastors to have to face a dialogue at the end of their sermons, where people could ask, "What did you mean by that, and what are its implications?"

Mr. Davis: I heard about a pastor who had preached a particularly interesting sermon one morning. As the people passed through the doors of the church, everybody came to him and shook hands and said, "Pastor, that was really beautiful; God bless you for it." Finally, one dear lady came to him, took his hand, and said, "You have been our pastor for 12 years, and you have preached the gospel to us. But when are you going to allow the Holy Spirit to give unction to your messages?" That lady had the courage to speak the truth to him. He said she made him realize that no matter how eloquent or entertaining he was, unless his messages were undergirded by the Spirit of God, they were just human words. And it changed his ministry.

Dr. Wiseman: Jim, you've put us ministers on the hot seat.

Mr. Davis: I didn't mean to attack anyone. In fact, the word *layman* offends me in some ways. I feel the Lord has given me a ministry of my own. The Apostle Paul says we are all apostles of Christ, and I feel the weight of my responsibility as strongly as you do. The counseling that I do at school and the Sunday school class that I teach and the Bible study class in our home are my "congregations." The Lord has led me to believe that all those things are His causes and I am merely His instrument.

Dr. Dobson, Jr.: I'm also a bit weary of the word *sharing*, which is overworked in describing the pulpit ministry. Shouldn't there be times when a pastor speaks with the power and authority of God's Word, instead of groping along in the darkness, mixing his opinions with ours? Sharing, to me, implies a human endeavor without much that could be called "divine inspiration."

Mr. Davis: I'd just like to share with you . . .

Dr. Cunningham: That's a reaction to the earlier error of "preaching down" to people. We have heard all through our training, "Don't preach down to people . . . include yourselves in." When you're talking about problems, they should be called "our problems." Instead of setting yourself on a pedestal for all to emulate, you're encouraged to admit that "I am also on a pilgrimage . . . a journey." I use that approach too. However, I think people sometimes wonder, Hasn't anybody ever arrived? Aren't there some definite conclusions that we can draw? Isn't there something we're not still wondering about?

Rev. Dobson, Sr.: Dogmatism and authority have almost disappeared from the ministry.

Mr. Davis: We are too careful along this line. Christian people are looking for truth and they are looking for absolutes. If they don't find them in the church, they will look elsewhere. This is one reason Bill Gothard has been so successful.

Dr. Dobson, Jr.: That fact is verified by the surveys showing which churches are growing. Those that stand for something are growing, and the bland, "anything goes" denominations are losing ground.

Mrs. Hull: May I say something in defense of "sharing"?

Dr. Cunningham: You go ahead and defend it.

Mrs. Hull: One of the finest pastoral relationships we ever had was with a young couple who had a beautiful ability to share. The wife would stand up on Wednesday night and say, "My son just drove me nutty today. He spilled his milk in the morning and made messes all day long. So during his nap-time, I just had to take the phone off the hook, get the Bible out, read and pray, and put myself in God's hands." The young mothers in our church immediately identified with her. You know, that meant something to me, too. Not only had we experienced the same frustrations, but she shared a solution we could all relate to. Dozens of people came to her for counseling and she was willing to say, "Yeah, I know what you mean; that is a problem; let's pray about it. We can talk about it and maybe we can both learn something."

Dr. Dobson, Jr.: Aarlie, that approach is extremely valuable and has a definite place in Christian service. My question is, however, Should that constitute the *sum total* of a pastor's ministry? Are there not other occasions when the minister's purpose is not to "share" mutual frustrations but to speak with authority about the immutable truths from God's Word?

Dr. Wiseman: It seems to me that somewhere we have to get in what I call the "incarnation ministry." Let me give you an example. My wife's mother had been in the hospital 50 days with terminal cancer. The day she died was really a dark day for me, and I was asking all kinds of basic questions. "Why at this point in our lives did this have to happen? What about the impact on our children?" I said to my college class of ministerial students that day, "Hey, somebody else is going to have to pray at the beginning of class this morning." One student prayed for the class, for himself, and for me. At the end of his prayer, another stood up and said, "There's something I want to tell you. I work on a machine at a factory from 11 p.m. to 7 a.m. I put my Greek verbs on three-by-five cards and tape them to the machine so I can memorize them while I work. But last night your name kept coming to my mind." This fellow was trying to say how much he cared for me and was assuring me that he was praying for me and my family. This matter of ministry is much deeper than sharing and relating mutual woes. It is standing where others stand and feeling what others feel.

Dr. Cunningham: Again, it's not "either/or." It's both. There must be a balance.

Rev. Dobson, Sr.: That's my point. I feel there has been an imbalance for the past 20 years. There is a time for deep, Christian empathy; but there is also a time to put the emphasis on the authority of God, if, in fact, you come with a message from the Lord. I have an evangelistic viewpoint, of course, but I could not go into a pulpit Sunday after Sunday and preach exclusively on love, when I knew that people were committing outright blasphemy of the name of God and denying everything that the Bible stands for. I just couldn't do it. I would feel compelled to remind my congregation that God is not a permissive grandfather who winks at sin and depravity.

Mr. Davis: I heard a missionary say that he had been speaking in Central America on an evangelistic campaign tour. Everywhere he went he preached on the love of Christ, His redemptiveness, the Good News, etc. But these natives lived in the coastal villages where the weather was warm, and they thought nothing of going nude on the beaches. There was immorality on a wide scale, as well as blasphemy of the name of God, and other evils. This missionary just couldn't get the idea of sin across to them. There was no genuine repentance. He was discussing this problem with members of his board of directors when one dear old gentleman suggested, "Distribute literature on the Ten Commandments." So everywhere they went, they distributed translations of the Ten Commandments in simple *Living Bible* language. It wasn't long before they had a genuine revival. These people, after reading the laws of God, began to see their needs and their sinful condition. God's Word will speak for itself if given an opportunity.

Dr. Dobson, Jr.: Sure it will, if given a fair hearing. Perhaps we have made our point on this subject, but I'd like to add one more comment: When a minister presents only the love of God, he makes it impossible for his congregation to understand the purpose of Jesus' life and death. The Messiah came to provide a *remedy* for a *disease*. That disease is called sin. If people are not taught the awful, vile nature of man's sinful state and God's hatred for it, then it is impossible for them to comprehend the miraculous remedy made available on the Cross.

In the same way, penicillin is nothing more than a sticky, gooey substance until we understand the meaning of bacterial infection. It is only when one comprehends the way bacteria can destroy the human body that antibiotics assume the significance of "miracle cures." It seems to me that many ministers have told their congregations that Jesus loves them, but deprived them of any true understanding of His most miraculous redemptive gift.

Mr. Davis: How can anyone argue with that?

Rev. Dobson, Sr.: And, coming back to what Jim

[Dobson, Jr.] said, family life would be strengthened by this more complete understanding of God's Word.

Dr. Dobson, Jr.: It would help us obey God, and obedience to His commandments produces harmony and love between people.

Ministries and Training Programs

Dr. Dobson, Jr.: Paul, you made a brief recommendation yesterday which we tabled at the time. Let's go back to your comment about the need for premarital and marital training sessions.

Dr. Cunningham: Well, it has occurred to me that problem marriages are usually the result of problem people . . . people with unresolved hang-ups who bring those frustrations into marriage, hoping that somehow marriage will resolve the difficulties they had as single individuals. It doesn't. Sometimes it maximizes those problems. So where do we start to help people to build the kind of homes that they want and need? I have come to believe that the teen-age years offer the best opportunity for this instruction, so that young people can move toward marriage with a healthier concept and a greater awareness of what marriage is and what it isn't. I think we should develop some first-rate training materials that would help us teach the principles of successful family living to late-adolescents.

Mrs. Hull: That is badly needed. Teen-agers are very romantic, even though they may not believe it. If they could just realize that marriage isn't a kind of Cinderella story . . . that it often involves a lot of hard work and sacrifice.

Dr. Hernandez: I don't know of a profession that is

lacking more in adequate preparation and training than that of child rearing and home management. We ought to spend much more time and energy in this area of instruction. And I think the high school level is the best place to begin. I've spoken to high school students at our church with some success. I have found if I take a smaller group of about 15 kids, that I accomplish more than if I try to talk to 60 or 80.

Dr. Cunningham: I think that's a valid point. The content involves personal issues that would probably "freeze" the discussion in a large group. The second desperate need at this point is to have a marriage enrichment program for those who have been married from one to three years (and longer). By that time, husbands and wives have begun to hit some of the thorny problems of marriage. Someone has said, "Marriage is the most difficult of all relationships to make work." If that's true, then we need to support the institution of marriage during its most stressful times.

Dr. Dobson, Jr.: Paul, maybe you're aware of the program initiated by the Catholic church, called Marriage Encounter. It has been enormously successful for the purpose you mentioned.

Dr. Hernandez: The Mormons have one, too.

Dr. Cunningham: Yes, those are "preventive programs," and I think the present crisis in marriage demands something like that.

Mrs. Hull: Just what goes on in Marriage Encounter?

Mr. Davis: All of my information on the subject is secondhand, but I can tell you what I've heard about it. They don't want "sick" marriages or those that are on the rocks. It's not a therapeutic kind of setting, but it is a program to get husbands and wives talking to each other again. As I understand it, they give assignments for couples to go off together for an hour and talk about things that are really important to each of them . . . to list the issues that each person cares about, etc. I think it's a program to focus attention on each other instead of the thousands of intereferences in family life. This is undoubtedly a very incomplete explanation.

Dr. Wiseman: Well, that sounds like something any church could easily do in many settings with minimal training.

Dr. Cunningham: They don't have much leadership training involved with it. They have weekend retreat-type seminars on a regular basis. One couple who is already part of the group will identify with a new couple that is coming into the group. That provides a vehicle for sharing enrichment procedure.

Dr. Wiseman: So it is really led by a couple who has been through the program earlier?

Dr. Cunningham: Yes, that's my understanding. These are the resource people within the group. Of course, there is also some leadership in addition to that.

Dr. Dobson, Jr.: Marriage Encounter involves a minimum of lecture and a minimum of theology and church dogma, but a maximum emphasis on communication. That's why it has been so highly effective. I haven't heard one criticism of the program.

Dr. Cunningham: Well, the point, again, is that the church can make a great contribution to the stability and effectiveness of marriage. Even good relationships need to be revitalized at times. One of the tremendous problems I hear about in marriage counseling, with women especially, is that they are often so bored. And boredom may just be marriage's greatest enemy. The success of Marabel Morgan's *Total Woman* concept

. . . even though some disagree with the book . . . is that she blasts through with the need to put a little excitement in marriage. I think a relationship that doesn't have some variety now and then is in trouble. And one way to make it exciting is for the partners to understand each other better and begin to look for ways to please one another. A good marriage enrichment program could help accomplish that.

Dr. Dobson, Jr.: You know, we're throwing out so much "unsolicited advice" to our readers that I'm afraid our recommendations are starting to blend together in a confusing array. But there is another suggestion that I want to make to churches which I feel is *extremely* important: The larger congregations should consider creating a staff position called Director of Women's Ministries. Women, today, need someone specifically trained in coordinating activities that help support their roles as wives and mothers.

Rev. Dobson, Sr.: Give an example.

Dr. Dobson, Jr.: Well, in the first place, the "bored" housewife Paul mentioned needs the love, support, and involvement of other Christian women. She needs a reason to get out of the house and mix with others who have the same spiritual commitment and home responsibility. She will profit from Bible studies, family training courses, a Valentine's banquet in February, etc. Those kinds of programs do not just happen unless someone has the responsibility to organize them. The reason I feel this is so vital is because women as a whole are agitated today. The feminine role has turned upside down, and many women seem to wonder who they really are and what they should be doing. Men seldom seek marriage counseling, initially. It's the women who come to say, "I'm depressed, discouraged, and lonely." A director of women's ministries could help alleviate many of those problems in a large church.

Dr. Cunningham: If a pastor's wife happens to be effective in this area, she can assume some of that kind of programming.

Dr. Dobson, Jr.: And your wife does.

Dr. Cunningham: Yes, she gives leadership in that area. A church has to arrange its priorities and decide just how big its staff can be.

Dr. Dobson, Jr.: I know it would be expensive to add a director of women's ministries, and most church budgets are already stressed. But because of the cultural changes occurring among women today, a pressing need has been created that has vast implications for the stability of the home. A church can provide a tremendous service by meeting that need.

Rev. Dobson, Sr.: Women's Bible study groups have sprung up all across the nation as a result of that need.

Dr. Dobson, Jr.: That's right, but I think we have fallen into a trap of limiting our program and services to the context of Bible studies. Perhaps this is not what Bible teachers want to hear, but my observation is that many women come to Bible studies not from a desire to memorize the Bible or to learn its technical aspects. Instead, they're there to figure out how to get through tomorrow morning. And I would like to see churches offer not only Bible studies, but also the kind of practical application of spiritual principles for family living that we have been talking about for two days. I find great frustration among women who go to Bible studies in hopes that they are going to get answers for the problems that they face, but they leave without those answers because the teachers fail to focus on what the Bible has to say about everyday needs. The

Word speaks directly about husband-and-wife relationships and sex and child rearing. These are very worthwhile subjects for study. Women want this help and we should accommodate them.

Dr. Cunningham: You seem to imply that women are the only ones who need those skills. It relates to what I have been talking about . . . this marriage enrichment kind of thing where both husbands and wives are involved.

Dr. Dobson, Jr.: Let me give two responses to that, Paul. First, husbands are working during the day. You can invite them, but they won't be there. If you have training sessions in the evening, there are family responsibilities that will limit the participation. You won't get half the crowd that would attend if scheduled in the morning. Women are free at ten o'clock in the morning when the kids are in school, and they want this kind of program. Secondly, there is much that can be done for women even if their husbands don't come. Women need to talk to each other and hear that their problems are not unique. They need to pray for one another and share answers to common problems. We obviously want to reach the men, too, but that is another assignment.

Dr. Cunningham: Yes, the women are open, they want help, but you're often dealing with stone-deaf husbands. How are we going to get to him? He's my main concern.

Dr. Dobson, Jr.: You may have to blast him on Sunday morning.

Mrs. Hull: My husband teaches a Sunday school class and he recently reviewed a couple of books, including yours, Jim, on how men should treat their wives. He gave specific examples and the women just ate it up and applauded. But afterwards, the men wouldn't even take the time to read the books. That's the way it is. Women are supposed to study and learn, but men are disinterested and unconcerned.

Dr. Dobson, Jr.: You know, Aarlie, sometimes Joyce Landorf and I split our Family Forum audiences by sex. When I talk to the men about the subject of my book, they sit there and bat their eyes as if to say, "What is the man saying to me?" But when I talk to the women about that subject, it's like putting a match to gasoline. I was interviewed on this subject last year on CBS radio in St. Louis. I talked about the needs of women and housewives and then we took live calls from listeners. The station made a tape recording of the program, and I wish you could hear the responses of the women who called in. It was just unbelievable. One woman called me, "Precious," . . . "that precious man," she said. I don't think I've ever been called "precious" before. Husbands often have no real understanding of the issues we were discussing.

Mrs. Hull: This is so prevalent. The men don't seem to care.

Dr. Dobson, Jr.: I think many of them *do* care, but they face ample frustrations and pressures of their own. Your husband used his Sunday school class for that purpose, and I wish other teachers were that sensitive to needs. I recently listed a few of the subjects that I thought should be covered regularly in every young married Sunday school class. Perhaps it would be helpful to teachers for me to include that list in the Appendix to this book.

Dr. Cunningham: We should spend a moment or two discussing the church's responsibilities to the unmarried.

Dr. Hernandez: Single adults represent one of the most frustrated segments of our society, not only in the church, but outside of it. They are in that twilight zone, neither in nor out. They are often at odds with themselves and others as well. So many seem to be starved for fellowship and may be the loneliest people in the church.

Dr. Cunningham: We have just added a staff member at our church this year with responsibility for singles. We have a tremendous group of unmarried adults, and we knew they were not being ministered to. I have also tried to give deserved pulpit recognition of their existence and importance. I've said, "We think our singles are very special, and you know the most important man who ever lived was single." Everyone needs to know that he is welcome and needed.

I know a college president who has chosen to be single, not because he dislikes marriage, but he has felt after consideration this was probably the best life-style for him. He spoke at the Continental Congress on the Family last year. He stressed the need for every single to become involved in the life of a family, in order to avoid selfishness. He said he has become a part of a family that has been open and warm and loving to him. He baby-sits for the parents because he feels that in order to be a whole person that he needed occasional contact with children. He said the only people in the world who ever hugged him and kissed him were children, and that every living person needs to be hugged and kissed by somebody. By giving to this family and filling in now and then, he avoided a welfare situation where all of the giving went one way. The family returned his love by inviting him to dinner on special days when singles are the most lonely . . . on Christmas and Thanksgiving and days like that.

You know, we try to organize and systematize everything in the church until the people get a little weary of all that programming. And yet, if you don't take some kind of direct approach to human needs, your efforts become merely good intentions that never materialize.

Dr. Dobson, Jr.: I suppose the central message within all our comments is that the church should not only *preach* the gospel . . . but it should help its people *live* the gospel in this stressful era.

Dr. Cunningham: Yes, and that requires some creative approaches to new situations.

Discipline in the Sunday School

Rev. Dobson, Sr.: Jim, I have heard you express some criticism of the Christian Church generally with regard to discipline and behavior in Sunday schools. It ought to be restated here.

Dr. Dobson, Jr.: Well, it has been my strong conviction that the church should support the family in its attempt to implement biblical principles in the home. This is especially true with reference to the teaching of respect for authority. This isn't an easy time to be a parent because authority has eroded drastically in our society. Therefore, mothers and fathers who are trying to teach respect and responsibility to their children, as the Bible prescribes, need all the help they can get, particularly from the church.

But in my opinion, the church fails *miserably* at this point. There is no aspect of the church mission that I feel is weaker or more ineffective than discipline in the Sunday school. Parents who have struggled to maintain order and respect all week send their kids off to church on Sunday morning, and what happens? They are permitted to throw erasers and shoot paper wads and swing on the light fixtures. This is particularly distressing to me. I am not referring to one denomination. I've seen it happen in almost all of them. In fact, I think I was one of those eraser throwers in my day.

Rev. Dobson, Sr.: Why do you think our Sunday schools are so lax and permissive?

Dr. Dobson, Jr.: Teachers are volunteers who may not know how to handle kids. But more importantly, they are afraid of irritating sensitive parents. They don't feel they have a right to teach children to respect God's house. If they try, they might anger Mama Bear and lose the entire family.

Dr. Cunningham: And they well could. That's the problem. People are so sensitive about their kids. I came through a permissive atmosphere in the Chicago public school system where a teacher was forbidden by law to touch a child. I mean they could not even *touch* a child . . . and the same restriction was put on the police department. I've seen kids in that city just stand and taunt policemen and dare them to do anything to them by threatening to sue. Everybody is so scared of lawsuits, you know, and are afraid to reprimand or punish someone else's child.

Dr. Dobson, Jr.: I'm not recommending that we spank kids in the Sunday school, of course. But there are ways to maintain order among children, once we decide that it is important to us. Training sessions can help teachers to do a better job. Pastors can back up Sunday school workers, etc. My concern is that we can't seem to agree that discipline has a place on Sunday morning. In its absence, the chaos that results is an insult to God and to the meaning of worship.

Mr. Davis: Paul, are you in favor of a permissive Sunday school?

Dr. Cunningham: No, I'm not! But we do have to be tactful and wise in dealing with people.

Mr. Davis: We may lose a few families by insisting that children behave themselves, but I think we would gain much more by supporting discipline and obedience and learning. People are searching for reasonable limits, and I believe they'll support a church that isn't afraid to stand up and be counted.

Dr. Hernandez: I read somewhere of a high school teacher who resigned from her position because it became unbearable. In her letter of resignation she said, "The teachers are afraid of the principal, the principal is afraid of the superintendent, the superintendent is afraid of the school board, and the school board is afraid of the parents, and the parents are afraid of the children, and the children are afraid of nobody."

Mr. Davis: There's some truth to that in my school district, too.

Rev. Dobson, Sr.: I was in a revival meeting in a packed house, some years ago, when a little kid came down the aisle right while I was preaching and began parading back and forth across the platform. I kept preaching as best I could. Finally he stood on his head. And just between sentences I said, "I hope he doesn't break his neck." (I almost wished he would, you know!) That really started a commotion. Those parents (who, by the way, were there for the first time) got so angry with me that they said they'd never come back. That's the kind of thing you're faced with.

Dr. Dobson, Jr.: I don't doubt that there would be a few families who might be insulted by being told that their child was not behaving properly. But my concern is that we will lose the complete effectiveness of the Sunday school by not requiring children to cooperate.

You can't teach anything in an atmosphere of chaos. You can't teach kids when they don't even hear you.

Dr. Cunningham: I couldn't agree with you more. We are trying to insist on discipline and obedience in our church Sunday program, and as Jim Davis said, I don't think we have to lose families by doing so. We are just obligated to deal with some children in more creative, meaningful ways . . . just like they have to do in the public school. We may remove a child from the setting or perhaps have a teacher assigned to him alone until he cools down. I would not want to say, "You can't come back to Sunday school," to any child. Instead, we will try to adapt. We will say, "We care so much about this child that we're going to go to whatever lengths are necessary to try to communicate God's Word to him. And so, parents, we wanted you to know how we are having to approach instruction of your child. We hope we have your support. We love this child and we care about him and we want him to make it. So when this kind of experience is no longer necessary, we'll reintroduce him to the classroom."

Dr. Dobson, Jr.: I like that, Paul.

Mr. Davis: There's one more aspect to this which is frightening to me. Aarlie has mentioned that she has very sharp children who are doing well in school. Kids like that can see the lack of discipline in the public schools and the lack of effort required of other children in the classroom. That produces a disrespect for educators and public schools. But the church should generate the opposite response. It ought to be a place which would make kids say, "I wish my school classroom was like that." Because it isn't, Beverly and I are having kids in our home who say, "I don't learn anything. Nothing's happening there." That really bothers me because the Sunday school deals with the most important issues in life; and if it fails, what agency will replace it?

Mrs. Hull: And it can contribute so much. You know, when our friend died, we talked to the children about how we were going to see him again in heaven. Our kids are getting old enough to understand eternal life, and I asked my little eight-year-old girl, "Heather, do you think you're going to see him?" And she kind of smiled and said, "That's what John (her Sunday school teacher) asked me." I then learned that they had discussed how Jesus had died but is alive again. Even though I've said it millions of times, John had said it again and she remembered exactly what he had said. And oh, I appreciated that so much.

Mr. Davis: That's backing up the home by what is being taught at church.

Mrs. Hull: Yes, and we need that support. I appreciate John because he obviously cares about those kids.

The Church's Interference in Family Life

Dr. Hernandez: We've talked about many subjects, but we need another week to cover all the relevant topics. I wish we had more time.

Dr. Cunningham: We have discussed some of the services the church can provide to strengthen family life. How about the other side of the coin? Are there areas in which the church might be destructive to the family?

Dr. Dobson, Jr.: There are occasions when the church is guilty of pulling husbands and wives away from their homes too many nights each week. This over-commitment must be an extremely common source of frustration among women, particularly, because it is mentioned to me so frequently when I am speaking or counseling. I have a note, here, which will explain what I mean. It was handed to me by a woman just prior to the start of a Family Forum Seminar last summer.

Dear Dr. Dobson,

I hope that you will take some time out during your talks to discuss the following problem. I know it isn't unique to me. I am at the point of tears as I write this because I fear for my marriage.

I love the Lord with all my heart and I want to serve Him more than anything. My husband I are actively involved in Christian work.

What I need to know is whether or not it is possible for a person to be too involved in Christian work. Our homelife as a family is being rapidly reduced due to our involvement in these activities. When I bring it to my husband's attention, he says it must be a spiritual problem on my part because we need to give our "all" to God. I agree, but doesn't God expect us to answer for the way our families turn out? I believe we are going to have to give account for how we raise them. I think that if we become too involved in *anything*, our children and spouse will suffer. In these days, when homes are falling apart, Christians should be on guard against this trap. It takes *both* a husband and wife being at home regularly to develop a homelife that is pleasing to God!

I imagine quite a few husbands will think their wives wrote this letter, because I know of several situations like mine. PLEASE, Dr. Dobson, help us! Give advice to us. We will listen to you.

I'm sorry I can't sign my name. I'm too self-conscious. I'm sure you'll understand.

Thank you.

Sincerely,

I believe this woman is right when she says this problem is shared by many other families. And the church must take some responsibility for alleviating it.

Dr. Hernandez: That's very true, Jim. In fact, when I

learned to say no, I felt the greatest personal emancipation . . . freedom to be able to say no. I will admit being vulnerable to guilt feelings that come when people ask me to do this or that, but there has to be a balance in responsibilities.

Dr. Cunningham: You never need to feel guilty about saying no to man; saying no to God is different.

Dr. Dobson, Jr.: I used to have the idea that anything the church requested me to do was like hearing an order from God. I just said yes to everything. That was 1964 when my daughter was not even born. During one busy stretch, I went 17 nights without being home, most of the time being spent in the work of the church. That's when I began to draw the conclusion that God expected me to use my common sense in the jobs that I accepted.

Mrs. Hull: Elton Trueblood said that he believed the church to be one of the greatest enemies of a Christian family. He told me that when I interviewed him personally. He refers to the children of overworked parents as "church orphans."

Dr. Dobson, Jr.: I would like to see pastors state from the pulpit that they don't want to interfere with family life. "Obviously the church cannot run without lay help, but don't let us destroy your family. When you can't give any more, say no to us."

Dr. Cunningham: May I also say, however, that some people use the church as an excuse . . . another dodge, another place to work, to get away from their families.

Dr. Wiseman: That's an important point. We can indict the church, whereas in some cases, if the parents were at home, it wouldn't change anything.

Dr. Dobson, Jr.: There's more than one way to shirk

your responsibility as a parent. The church can't be blamed for many of them.

Mr. Davis: You know, there never do seem to be enough women to handle the primary and elementary Sunday school classes. I wish we could make a specific pitch for more men to get involved at that level. We have several situations in our church where couples handle the younger classes. In one of them, the husband is called "Papa Bear" by the kids, and they really love that guy.

Dr. Dobson, Jr.: Many young children have almost no contact with men . . . particularly those from broken homes. I believe if pastors would make a specific appeal from the pulpits and explain the reason men are needed, they'd get some takers. We are just so culturally oriented toward women working with small children.

Mrs. Hull: That's certainly worth a try.

Music in the Church and Home

Rev. Dobson, Sr.: There's a matter that I feel we should discuss, but I am reluctant to bring it up because I have such strong feelings on the subject. I'm referring to the status of church music today. In fact, we probably ought to discuss this "off the record," because I don't want to appear unduly critical of groups or individuals in the church.

Dr. Dobson, Jr.: Does the subject relate to family life? Do trends of church music tie in with the theme of our book?

Rev. Dobson, Sr.: I feel that it certainly does relate.

It is extremely important that we advocate, endorse, and hold up for emulation *in the church* the same principles that we are fighting for *around the family fireside.*

Mrs. Hull: What do you mean?

Rev. Dobson, Sr.: I feel that throughout evangelical Christianity, we have allowed the music of the church to be influenced too much by the so-called rock culture.

Mrs. Hull: In what way?

Rev. Dobson, Sr.: Rock music is not only a succession of sounds presented in a certain manner, but it has become a *symbol* of antichristian values . . . a vehicle which promotes sexual promiscuity, infidelity, drug addiction, and the general flood of ungodliness that true Christians are opposed to everywhere. The thing that disturbs me is that in many churches those in charge of the music have allowed the worship service to become invaded by the spirit, the mannerisms, the terrific amplification, the beat, the dress, and the choreography that bespeaks the basic character of rock music. That to my mind is highly inconsistent.

Mrs. Hull: He believes it!

Rev. Dobson, Sr.: I think you will too, Aarlie, if I can make you see what I really mean. In a nutshell, I believe we are obligated to teach our people that there is a difference between true worship and sensuous entertainment. Instead we have allowed the distinction to erode.

Dr. Cunningham: Do you find this an increasing or decreasing phenomenon?

Dr. Dobson, Jr.: I think the so-called acid rock is to some degree on the decrease in today's music, but the broader category of rock music in recent years seems to have become acceptable in the church.

Mr. Davis: So much of the kids' music is more like noise than melodies and songs. I heard of a waiter in a nightclub who dropped a huge tray of dishes . . . and everyone got up and started dancing.

Rev. Dobson, Sr.: Some of the groups performing in the church have all of the identifying features of secular rock groups. If they were on television and you turned the sound off, you would be hard pressed to tell one from the other. And it really bothers me when they seem to equate Christian joy with the senseless twisting and shaking accompanied by ear-splitting sound.

Dr. Dobson, Jr.: Whenever a touring teen-age group comes into the church, one of the first things you'll notice is the tremendous amount of electronic equipment they use. And hanging from the ceiling will be large banks of colored lights with which to produce a psychedelic effect. Now, there's nothing inherently evil about electronic devices or lighting equipment, but again, the model for this approach has been the very worst of the youth culture. And to me, it doesn't have much to do with worship.

Dr. Cunningham: Well, if you operate your worship program on an entertainment basis, there will eventually be a payday. If it's built on an entertainment principle, then you have to keep making it bigger and better, because people become satiated. Also, few churches can compete with commercial television on a technical level. Most of the time we come out looking rather sad by comparison—chiefly because we're amateurs and they're pros.

However, religion doesn't have to be boring. We have tried to maintain what I consider to be a conservative and hopefully a balanced approach to music programming. Sometimes we can enjoy humor, we can laugh, we can feel good, we can respond to what is happening in a worship service, provided it is an inspired happening. There must be a divine dimension for it to be a valid worship experience. But the sensuous music you mentioned represents the worst of the world; bringing that into the church is a mistake. However, I think it is a changing scene because the culture is beginning to turn away from acid rock, and I believe the church will soon do the same.

Rev. Dobson, Sr.: Time magazine of December 29, 1975, gives an unbelievable report on the current brand of popular music, call it by whatever name you will. It has an exceedingly vile influence on our youth; and far from "backing off," it now occupies 15 percent of all radio broadcasting time . . . and is growing astronomically, and I quote:

SEX ROCK

While television cameras rolled, the Rev. Charlie Boykin of Tallahassee, Fla., set fire to $2,000 worth of rock records. He did the same thing a month ago after learning that a poll of North Florida high schools revealed 984 of the 1,000 unmarried girls sampled had become pregnant listening to pop songs . . . during fornication, of course. Next month he plans to take his protest to Pansey, Ala. Actually, he might just as well burn the air waves. Just a twist of the AM dial demonstrates how far things have gone. On the average, 15% of air time is devoted to songs like "Do It Any Way You Wanna," "Let's Do It Again," "That's the Way I Like It," and "I Want'a Do Something Freaky to You." Radio's hottest song right now is also the most lubricous: "Love to Love You, Baby," Donna Summer's marathon of 22 orgasms.

Yummy Yummy. Boston-born Donna, a former singer in the German production of *Hair*, who has been singing and modeling in Europe for the past eight years, wrote the lyrics herself. They are stunningly simple . . . mostly five words repeated 28 times. Donna's message is best conveyed in grunts and groans and languishing moans. Her goal is to make an album "for people to take home and fantasize in their minds." First she fantasized all alone in a dark studio, listening to the song's prerecorded track. "I let go long enough to show all the things I've been told since childhood to keep secret." She and her promoter, Neil Bogart, the president of Casablanca Records (previous hits: "Chewy, Chewy," and "Yummy, Yummy Yummy, I've Got Love in My Tummy"), are being hailed as the sex rock pioneers.

Their profits can only grow. Radio's electronic orgasmatron shows no signs of exhaustion. Only nine years ago, the Rolling Stones had trouble getting "Let's Spend the Night Together" on the air. But that was before radio became the billion-dollar record industry's top sales force.

The article goes on to tell how songs are selected:

Nothing can be left to chance. At Preview House in Los Angeles, new songs are tested before a demographically selected group of 400 teen-agers. As each number is played, the kids turn their dials between Very Dull and Very Good. Some seats are equipped with "basal skin response sensors," to measure the involuntary spasms of the nervous system. "An orgasm sound never fails to produce a sharp spike in the BSR response," says Larry Heller, music director of Preview House.

Dr. Cunningham: That's a depressing article! But the subtle thing is that some of those quotes are not referring to the hard rock *sound*. That's what I meant before. Now they are beginning to put these dirty, filthy *words* together with a lilting melody. We think the alarm is over . . . but this is more dangerous because they're more compelling . . . the tunes are pretty again.

Rev. Dobson, Sr.: Yeah, they are calling this new one *orgasmic rock*.

Dr. Wiseman: But on the other hand, you have to take into consideration that sometimes a whole congregation is made up of an arty type of people . . . maybe they have been saved from the depths of a culture like you have been describing and maybe they don't know anything else. So when they accept Christ, they naturally worship God in the only cultural idiom they know. I have seen and had experience with people like this and have heard them witness and it is genuine. Let me give you an example. I know a woman who was a barroom pianist for maybe 20 years. This was the way she made her living before she was beautifully converted. Now she plays the piano for a church congregation, and she has the most far-out chords that you ever heard in your life. And when I hear those chords I have to say, "That's strange to my ears, but that is the testimony to what she is and what God has helped her to become." Incidentally, the whole congregation where she worships has been almost totally immersed in that culture. Now where do culture and Christianity collide? I suppose we can't handle such a question in this book. But let's not be too hard on those people!

Dr. Dobson, Jr.: I agree; we ought to be patient with others and be careful not to criticize those whose tastes are different from our own. But neither should a special case like that become a norm for all the rest of the church. God and Christianity are not at war with any cultural idiom . . . only with the evil elements it may contain. And when someone becomes a Christian, he separates himself from those aspects of his culture which are contradictory to a Christian way of life. The rock culture, quite *apart from its music*, represents the grossest immorality! I'm sure everyone is familiar with the concept of "groupies" . . . young girls who follow musical troupes around. They will have sex with any musician just so long as he is in a band . . . drug usage, whatever is filthy, whatever is rotten, the rock culture represents it. Therefore, I think there is great danger in getting too close to it in symbolism and words and manner and movement and in dress and in volume. For the same reason, its leaders are not fit subjects for emulation by Christian young people.

Dr. Wiseman: I know there are evils connected with the rock culture. I'm not for it either, and there are other aspects of the music that don't make any sense to me; but this expression has more significance and meaning to some people than it does to me. I heard a lecture on church music at the seminary in which a speaker, Don Hustad, an authority in church music, made the statement that in the history of the church there has been no time when its music has been more than 200 years from the barroom. That was a completely new idea to me. He took some of the most moving elements in church music and began to illustrate his point. There was a time, for instance, that "Jesus, Lover of My Soul," was considered too sensuous to be sung in church. I can't imagine a hymnal without that beautiful number in it.

Dr. Hernandez: I don't quite understand your point.

Dr. Wiseman: My point is simply that church music has come from the context of the world throughout its history. I think we ought to call to mind this development of hymnology in our discussion so that our statements would be accurate.

Rev. Dobson, Sr.: I am sure you are right about that. Many sacred hymns and many of the great classical compositions as well were derived from popular tunes and folk songs, but it is a matter of opinion whether church music has gained anything by borrowing the rock idiom. I know that with it has come a cheapening and vulgarizing of music, music that formerly was filled with majestic beauty. Perhaps it's out of place to talk here about church music as *art,* but since Neil has turned the conversation in that direction, may I share something with you. I wrote a statement recently which reflects my personal views. I promise these will be my last words on this subject:

First, the *"poetry"* or *lyrics* to which many of today's musical compositions are set is of the most empty, vacuous, and artless kind, made up for the most part of catch phrases and formless jingles repeated endlessly; they waste nothing on the fear and reverence due the matchless name of God; they express no revulsion for the tragedy of sin. Both the songwriter and singer often join in a careless disregard for *doctrinal accuracy!* References to Christ and sacred themes are often presented in the tongue-in-cheek manner of the so-called country music style, which never made a pretense of being anything but fun and entertainment. (Witness how "western music" often presents on the same program a ribald song relating the antics of a drunk, alternated with an emotionalized rendering of "The Old Rugged Cross.")

The grace of God is often presented as compatible with the indulgent permissiveness of the age. God is represented as an extremely bland and spineless grandfather to whose name they owe no reverence; they address Him as an equal in overfamiliar language! All this to the pounding of drums and the electronic twanging of guitars! It seems incredible that there are so many who profess to see no contradictions in placing the awe-inspiring truths of the Bible in such a setting. This speaks eloquently, or so it seems to me, of the mental and spiritual vacuity of our times!

Let me add that what I've written here is a generalization: In fairness to our musicians, we could say that there are many exceptions.

Dr. Dobson, Jr.: I can hear a strong rebuttal coming back from those of the opposite opinion. Let me put on record the primary argument that we have all heard: "This is the music of *youth*. The reason you don't like it may be because you are older and are out of touch with the kids. And if young people get spiritual help from it, then why not?

Dr. Wiseman: They have a point. Why should we try to bind them to the mores of the past? Our not liking the impact of their culture is insufficient reason for condemning it. And if this kind of music has such tremendous drawing power, why should we not use it for the glory of God?

Mr. Davis: As I see it, there is a danger in going too far in that direction. I know that it is popular and that it draws people, but holding to convictions will always cost you something in the way of popularity. I believe this controversy will fall into its proper place if everything we do is done to the glory of God and is not done to the glory of man. We expect our ministers to preach under the anointing and unction of the Holy Spirit. Have we the right to expect the same of our musicians? Could we not recommend that pastors say to those who have charge of the special music, "Would you fast and pray that God would use your ministry of music . . . that He would help you to sing under the anointing of the Spirit?" This would help musicians understand that their efforts are to be to the glory of God . . . and not to be done in the spirit of entertainment.

Dr. Dobson, Jr.: That is more important to me than the quality of the music! There have been occasions when I have enjoyed hearing an untrained voice more than a highly skilled one, because of the spirit it conveyed.

Mr. Davis: In our church, the music committee lets musicians know several weeks in advance when they are going to sing or perform. I think that is the ideal way.

Dr. Dobson, Jr.: Let me say by way of wrap-up that I recently discussed this same topic of church music with one of the best-known singers in Christian music today. He would probably prefer that I not quote him by name. However, he cautioned me against any stance that would inhibit the expression of musical tastes unless clear moral issues are involved. Something which communicates nothing to one person might be meaningful to another. Furthermore, he pointed out that there is no single definition of "rock music," and we cannot naively assume that everyone understands what we mean by the term. I understand his point of view, although I feel that "clear moral issues" *are* involved in many aspects of today's music.

Mr. Davis: Before we leave the subject of music, can we spend a moment or two talking about music in the home?

Dr. Cunningham: I think a lot of the negative things we have said about what is happening to music in church stems from a lack of parental supervision in the home. The kind of music the kids are allowed to listen to and the kind of entertainment they see has a direct bearing on the local music programming in the church. As Jim [Dobson, Sr.] said earlier, we ought to be supporting the same values through our standards at home and in our services at church.

Mr. Davis: I hope we have made parents see how vital it is for them to "tune in" to the kind of filth their kids may be getting through recordings, and through radio and TV. We can't lay all the blame on the church. Many parents are too busy or they simply don't care!

Mrs. Hull: We have friends who had trouble with one of their girls in the drug culture. They said, "We should have seen it coming when she suddenly started dressing like kids of that group. We should have known it when she started wearing those bleached-out Levis and began picking up the other symbols of the drug culture." These things, along with the music, have become a kind of badge of their world.

Dr. Wiseman: If you are going to take bleached-out Levis off the college campuses, we're going to have some severe clothing problems.

Dr. Cunningham: I think what Aarlie's friend meant was that if the mother had been more perceptive, these things would have been a cue to her of what was going on and she could have done something about it . . . maybe.

Dr. Wiseman: On the positive side, I think we ought to state that music in the home is a good way to teach the orthodox faith.

Mrs. Hull: Oh, and to make use of the scripture music that is available now! Kids learn scripture by singing it in neat ways. My youngest girl loves some of the latest tapes, especially, "Ask, Seek, Knock"; that's her favorite song. We all love it.

Dr. Cunningham: The strength of these statements comes, in my opinion, from the laymen: from Jim Davis, Jim Dobson, Jr., from David, from Aarlie. Because many people would expect Jim, Sr., and Neil and myself to be opposed to this kind of music, since we are ministers.

Mr. Davis: I'll take credit for all of Rev. Dobson, Sr.'s, quotes. I agree with everything he said.

The Power of One
Christian Family

Dr. Dobson, Jr.: David, it would be a shame to end these discussions without hearing some of the circumstances of your early homelife and how your parents contributed to the man you are today. Your family has *lived* the principles we have been recommending, even though your parents faced hardship and poverty. It is appropriate that we conclude our effort with what I believe is a beautiful example of what we have been trying to express for two days.

Dr. Hernandez: Well, let me say first that I've been blessed by what I have been hearing today. I met most of you for the first time yesterday, and yet there is a common bond of beliefs and love for God which I feel with each of you. It's amazing to me; we come from such diverse backgrounds. I was raised in a very poor economic environment, as Jim said. My dad had only a third grade education. We lived under trees. Many times our furniture was just fruit boxes and I came through ghettos, and that kind of thing. But because of our fellowship in Jesus Christ, I sense a love and a oneness with each of you.

Dr. Dobson, Jr.: As a place to begin, let me ask you a specific question: The traditional way of studying the human personality is to look at people who develop emotional problems and character disorders. We've been trying to learn what causes them to collapse and fail. But more recently, I've been reading of research on the opposite kind of person . . . those people who succeeded in spite of every disadvantage. You were one of those kids who refused to be handicapped by poverty and hardship. The odds against your becoming a physician were enormous. Would you tell us how you were able to overcome the limitations of your environment? Where did you get your academic desire, and what was there about your homelife that contributed to the man we see today?

Dr. Hernandez: Well, I'll tell you, as far as my childhood was concerned, I had godly parents . . . parents who really loved me and the other kids. They were more concerned about my welfare than what they put on their backs. Material things were at the lowest level on their list of priorities. Our happiness and our education and our love for the Lord were at the highest level in our lives, and we were bathed in this aura of dignity . . . the dignity that comes from knowing that we are created in the image of God himself. Because of this training, we were able to rise from the ghetto and use our potential. My parents accepted our weaknesses and emphasized our strengths, and this is essentially where our confidence came from. There were other children in the neighborhood who had the same intellectual potential, but who didn't make it.

Dr. Cunningham: How were your parents converted?

Dr. Hernandez: Well, Mom came from Catholicism and so did Dad. In fact, Dad was the eldest of 18 children. My grandfather was a bootlegger and a very good one at that. He had a lot of money, but he spent most of it getting released from jails. My mom and dad were introduced to the Lord through neighborhood missionaries who had little meetings and gatherings to evangelize the children. They had no personal knowledge of Jesus Christ until then . . . no comprehension of His love.

Mr. Davis: How many children were in your family?

Dr. Hernandez: There were four children. My mom and dad were married in Arizona when they were both 17 years of age. They originated from Mexico, and I was born (their first child) in Phoenix, Ariz., October 29, 1937. Those were difficult times toward the end of the depression. Dad was not an American citizen, and therefore he couldn't get a job in the United States. Furthermore, he only had a third grade education and no one would hire him.

By the time I was three, things became very tough for us. My mom was pregnant with my sister, Delia, and we had gone for days without any food. Dad couldn't find a job of any kind. However, he was very proud and he never depended on anyone for anything. He just felt he and Mom were responsible for their family and they wouldn't beg or try to get a handout. But out of desperation, they decided that perhaps they ought to go to the governor of Arizona in the hopes that he could help Dad get a job. So they went to the capitol building in Phoenix, Ariz., and sat on the lawn with other peasants waiting out there. They knew the chief of state had to come out for lunch some time. So there's Mom, far along in her pregnancy, and I was three years old . . . rather dehydrated, they tell me.

About noontime, the governor and his entourage came out. Dad and Mom were sitting on a park bench awaiting as the official neared. Dad stood up and approached the governor, Robert Taylor Jones, and in broken English said, "I want you to give me a job. I don't have any food for my child. I don't want you to give me money; just give me a job." Governor Jones was stunned! The guards started to grab my dad and everyone became tense. But the whole thing settled down when the governor handed Dad a $10.00 bill, which in those days would be equivalent to $40.00 or $50.00 now. He told my dad to go and buy some food and come back the next day to work on the grounds as a gardener.

Three months later my dad was in a business for himself. He eventually owned a small lumber and adobe brick company and Mom started out with a little grocery store. It appeared that they had made it. They were financially sound. They had paid all their bills and their home was very comfortable. But then we underwent certain struggles. There were three children in the family by that time (Delia, Norma, and me), and my mother became pregnant with our brother. The pregnancy was complicated by a placenta implanted in the wrong direction. This caused constant bleeding and hospitalization, and the baby died. All funds began to be depleted. Soon after that crisis, my sister Delia developed a skin disorder that took my parents to Los Angeles, Mexico City, and other places in search for a solution or diagnosis or a treatment for her. The skin would peel off her face and it would bleed, leaving a raw base.

Finally, all the family resources were gone. We were completely bankrupt and decided to move to California because one of the Mexican doctors told us that a change of climate would be good for my sister. We loaded all our possessions in an old Ford truck and headed across the desert. I well remember that we didn't have any food with us, except for beans and a crate of watermelons, which had been given to us by my dad's friend. Today, you can fly from Phoenix to Los Angeles in 45 minutes and it takes only six hours to drive, but it took us six days to make the trip. That old truck broke down repeatedly, and we sat by the side of the road eating beans and watermelons in the desert. It is a miracle that our gastrointestinal tracts sustained the diet.

But anyway, we finally made it to Los Angeles and we were anxious to see the ocean for the first time. We had no place to shower or clean ourselves, so we headed straight for the great Pacific Ocean. Delia's face was still scaly and raw at that time. For months she had worn little metal gloves so she could not scratch or injure herself. I remember my agitation and despair as I watched her being taunted and teased by other children for the way she looked. Anyway, we bathed ourselves in the ocean and a miracle took place. Two days later, Dee's skin condition cleared up, and she's never had a problem since. To this day, we do not know how or what happened.

Dr. Dobson, Jr.: Were your parents committed Christians at that time, Dave?

Dr. Hernandez: Oh, yes. Many times we would just huddle around the old Spanish Bible, and I remember my parents' tears splashing on the pages. They trusted the Lord completely.

Rev. Dobson, Sr.: Do you suppose there was a chemical in the water that helped your sister?

Dr. Hernandez: I've tried to research it, but I still don't know what occurred. It was obviously a miracle. About that time we realized the potato season was in full swing in Bakersfield, so we went there. Of course, we didn't have a home or anything. We situated ourselves under a tree. My dad picked up about eight fruit trays which were used to dry fruit, and he put them up on one side. This was our home . . . no electricity, no running water, dirt floor, the open sky for a ceiling. Then he went to the dump and got an oil barrel, filled it half full with dirt, and cut a window for placing wood into it. This is where we cooked our beans and tortillas. That was our home for four months. We would pick potatoes from 6:00 in the morning till 6:00 in the evening.

In a short time Dad had saved enough money to buy a better truck. We picked up all our furnishings (a bunch of boxes that were turned over for beds) and took our oil barrel with us and moved to a tent for another six months. Finally, we moved to San Jose, Calif., where we were living in a converted chicken coop. Mom went to the back areas of grocery stores and brought home strips of cardboard which she used for wallpaper. Then she went to the Salvation Army and got some cheap water paints to decorate the walls. We really thought we were in great shape because this was the first time we had lived in a house. It was about a month later that the *San Jose News* labeled our street a "blighted area" of San Jose. We were stunned. We thought we had finally made it, you know.

We struggled a great deal during those years. Everything was sacrificed to make sure we children got a good education. And when I graduated from the eighth grade, I received a scholarship to go to the Brown Military Academy. I was to meet the dean of the academy at the St. Francis Hotel in San Francisco, but the week before that, my mom and dad took me for a ride around Santa Cruz to give me their final counseling session.

Dr. Dobson, Jr.: How old were you?

Dr. Hernandez: I was 13. As we were driving, I saw a sign that said, "The Monterey Bay Academy." It caught my eye. I thought it was a military academy. We came to find out it was a coeducational institution run by the Adventist denomination. We met the principal and a week later I was en route there instead of to the Brown Military Academy. I can still remember my parents' old '37 Chevy chugging into the distance after they dropped me off. It was the first time I had ever been away from home, and I remember the tremendous loneliness that came over me as I stood there on that campus, knowing no one except the principal. I was crying. For the first few weeks, I walked in my sleep and cried and wrote letters and called home every day. I later learned that my mom and dad stopped two or three times on the way home, almost ready to come back and pick me up. I thank the Lord that they didn't, because it was a tremendous experience. I learned to be independent from my parents during that time, and yet I depended more on the Lord than ever before.

From there I went on to college and to medical school, where I graduated in the upper percentage of my class. I am currently one of seven associates in a medical practice with a specialty in obstetrics and gynecology. Since 1969, I have been director of the Department of Community Medicine at White Memorial Medical Center and serve on the faculty of USC School of Medicine. We have approximately 75 interns and residents who are training with us at the present time. I tell you these facts to stress the way God has blessed my life so generously.

Dr. Dobson, Jr.: David, you've faced some other difficult moments in the past few years. I think you should share your personal crisis with us.

Dr. Hernandez: You're referring to the most overwhelming experience of my life. It began in January, 1974, when I first noticed a strange feeling of fatigue. I was extremely busy at that time, and I rationalized that I was merely working too hard. I had been extraordinarily healthy throughout my life, and I couldn't conceive of any serious illness striking me at 37 years of age. But then in March, I began to experience nausea about 45 minutes after each meal, and I had to consider the possibility of a physical disorder. I sought out a good specialist and we began the tedious task of identifying the problem. I underwent numerous blood tests and X rays, which revealed a dysfunction of the gall bladder and the liver.

Dr. Dobson, Jr.: Did you believe yourself to be seriously ill at that time?

Dr. Hernandez: No, because I had none of the pain, fever, or the jaundice that often go with serious illness. Likewise, the physicians were puzzled by this medical picture. So they called in the surgeons who decided, with my concurrence, to do an exploratory operation and remove my gallbladder. I was willing to part with my gallbladder rather than give up Mexican food. However, when they were into the surgery and examined my internal organs, they found a mass of scar tissue at the base of the common bile duct, which is the main drainage tube from the liver. The surgeons made a tentative diagnosis of sclerosing cholangitis and informed me of this fact when I awoke from the three-and-one-half-hour surgery.

I asked my surgeon to loan me the medical literature on this subject, and he gave it to Marilyn, somewhat reluctantly. He knew that if he didn't grant my request, that I would just have my secretary research it. But for several days, my wife avoided the issue and wouldn't let me see the reports. She had read the ominous studies and she offered various "excuses" to explain her refusal to bring the articles. She said, "Your sister has the literature," and "I left it downstairs." By the third day I demanded, "Look, Sweetheart. Let me have the material." She brought it to my bed.

I perused the studies and rapidly comprehended the reason for everyone's reluctance. I had known what to expect, but somehow the truth had not penetrated. I had not accepted it. But now, the evidence of medical experience was staring me in the face. I had a very serious disease with a sinister prognosis. My longevity was foreshortened by every medical indicator. As I began to face the reality of tragedy and its implications, a great cloud came over me. My life was in jeopardy, and I knew it.

About this time, Pastor Earl Lee visited my bedside. But I was at a point of despair. I was marooned . . . shipwrecked . . . on an island, believe me. I felt abandoned by God and dismayed by the rapid turn of events. As my pastor prayed, I just pleaded with God for mercy, but the long nightmare was just beginning. I found myself going through sleepless nights, trying to explain in rational terms the senselessness of this disease and suffering. All of the familiar questions occurred: Why me? Why our family? Why a loving God would permit this. You see, self-pity became the door to despair. And then bitterness and resentment set in, and I was becoming enslaved by my honest quandary. I thought of our two little boys growing up without a father. I thought of my wife struggling to make it alone. And I had strange dreams where I would awaken in a grave . . . helpless, unable to participate, unable to share, and unable to rejoice with the living.

It suddenly became clear to me that all my medical expertise couldn't save me. My physician friends and associates and all my connections in the medical world were powerless to change the prognosis. My competent surgeon couldn't alter the situation. My insurance policies couldn't grant me an extension on life. My financial investments couldn't offer me a reprieve. My professionalism and prestige meant nothing . . . absolutely nothing! I was stripped of all my securities. These earthly measures have their place and are useful, but they are not bulwarks. They were not worthy of my trust. Nothing can insulate us at a time like that. I found myself completely at the mercy of Almighty God!

Marilyn and I turned to the Lord for help. We cried and prayed and pleaded with the Lord for more faith. And our many Christian friends rallied to our support during that time. Our pastor, our family, our loved ones around the country . . . they were all so gracious and kind to us. A few days later, Jim [Dobson, Jr.] called me and shared the love of God. He said, "Dave, we are surrounding you with a wall of prayer!" A prayer and fasting chain was initiated by members of our Sunday school class. Marilyn and I were carried, literally, across a deep chasm on the wings of loving prayer.

On the fourth postoperative day, my mom and dad had to return to the Bay area. Before they left, my dad prayed for me in Spanish. I'll never forget that prayer. He said, "Almighty God, we present to You our son. Our *only* son! This son whom we love so much! We don't understand why he is suffering this affliction." As he continued to pray, I could read his mental anguish and his honesty with God. He was leaning over the railing, clutching my hand, and large, warm tears were splashing on my arm. Then he prayed, "Dear God, neither do we understand why You would give Your only beloved Son to die and redeem humanity." And I sensed at that moment a release . . . a transition into peace and understanding. The darkness began to dissipate. I came to terms with my limitations and my utter dependence on God. I accepted the Truth, and the Truth set me free.

Outward circumstances are no longer the determining factor in the degree of my happiness. My life is centered on God and His will, and I'm living one day at a time in humble dependence on Him. I now see the preciousness of time . . . of my wife and children and loved ones. This new perspective has eliminated the nagging disturbances which now seem so insignificant and inconsequential in the light of God's opportunities for an abundant life.

I still don't know what the future holds for me. I have wrestled with the Lord like Jacob of old, who told the angel at dawn, "I will not let you go until you bless me." Whether God's blessing on my life comes in the form of physical healing, or spiritual renewal, or just the peace that passes all understanding . . . that is *His* business. We are simply depending on Him to do the unusual, that His name would be glorified. I'm convinced that His plan is better than my plan, and I'm in His loving care.

Dr. Dobson, Jr.: Do you still fear death?

Dr. Hernandez: This was my first direct encounter with death. Of course, I had witnessed death many times in my patients because I do a lot of cancer work. But I had never confronted death myself. The Grim Reaper had never come that close to me . . . now I had to face him personally. More importantly, I had to decide whether or not I believed in a life after death. So many of us talk about eternal life, but I had to ask myself, Is this a myth or is it reality? Do I

167

really believe that there is a life for me beyond the grave? Will I really see my parents and my wife and my children in heaven? Will I really have an eternity with the Lord Jesus Christ. And I came to the conclusion after agonizing over this, that yes, life after death was awaiting me. And ever since then, all fear has gone. I no longer fear death, and I must tell you that physicians are not immune to death. They are not immune to the fear of death. In fact, we sometimes fear it more because we know what precedes it in many situations. But I no longer fear that. And so it's been a beautiful experience for me.

Mrs. Hull: Do you have fear for your family?

Dr. Hernandez: No, they are in His hands, too.

Dr. Dobson, Jr.: There's an extremely important message in what Dave has said: His greatest spiritual growth occurred during this lowest point in his life. I wish all of us could remember that when our personal crises come. Gold is purified by the refiner's fire.

Dr. Hernandez: I'll never forget what Neil Strait once wrote: "If you don't walk through the wilderness with the Lord Jesus, you'll never come out of the wilderness." That has made a tremendous impact on my life. I have been through the wilderness. If I'm going to come through this thing okay, I dare not turn loose of Jesus' hand.

Dr. Dobson, Jr.: Are your parents still praying for you?

Dr. Hernandez: They certainly are.

Dr. Dobson, Jr.: How old are they now?

Dr. Hernandez: Dad is 56, and Mom is 57.

Dr. Dobson, Jr.: Are they a source of strength for you even today?

Dr. Hernandez: There is no question about it. I am constantly aware of their love, and I feel the effects of their prayers in my life. I am grateful for the foundation of faith they instilled within me. I am also blessed by a wonderful wife, Marilyn, who gave me great strength and courage during those difficult days. Without this support of my loving family, I would not have made it through my crisis. Ultimately, however, only the Lord can give peace and quiet and rest when tragedy strikes.

Dr. Dobson, Jr.: Do you know what occurs to me, with a certain amount of shame? If I had seen that little Mexican-American family camped in poverty under a tree . . . amidst fruit-box furniture and an oil drum stove . . . if I had looked at those dirty children returning from 12 hours work in the potato fields . . . if I had seen Delia's flaky, scaly little face, and her dehydrated brother, I doubt if I would have believed even God could raise them up and pour out His love on them. But there, sitting on the dusty ground was a little fellow whom the Lord had chosen to bless. There was a future physician who would be loved by his patients and admired by his colleagues. And the most inspiring thought of all is that the vehicle for that blessing was a loving, stable family which put God first and trusted totally in Him, despite their poverty and struggles. His parents gave him a heritage that held him securely during the storm . . . despite the most difficult adversity that life can throw at a person.

Dr. Cunningham: What an eloquent testimony to everything we have been talking about here for two days!

Dr. Dobson, Jr.: You know, I've had the impression for several weeks, if not longer, that God had personally ordained what was about to take place here. That impression has grown during the last few days. He has a purpose for bringing us together for these discussions. And I really hope you all will pray for me as I try to edit what we've said, because the Christian family needs us. They need the encouragement of this message. It has been meaningful to me, and should be conveyed to others.

Dr. Wiseman: Well, these two days have been a means of bringing God's grace to me. Jim [Dobson, Jr.] and I had a few minutes alone together at lunchtime, and I told him that these last three weeks have been the toughest time in parenting that I've ever had in my life. I've gone through some personal problems that almost kept me from coming. I kept saying to myself, "What are you doing this for?" But so many things have fallen into place for me in these last few days, and I'm grateful to all of you for your ministries in my life.

Rev. Dobson, Sr.: I want to say something. I know that I have seemed quite vehement on several occasions during the past two days. I suppose these discussions have given me an opportunity to ventilate some frustrations that I've had no other occasion or means of expressing. You see, I don't have an outlet . . . the proper outlet for these concerns. I can't seem to do anything about them. But I love my church and I love each one of you.

Dr. Dobson, Jr.: That's precisely what I had in mind when I asked you to serve on this committee. Your viewpoint needs to be heard in the Christian community. Jim [Davis], do you have any last comment?

Mr. Davis: Praise the Lord. It's just beautiful to be here. I can't identify completely with Dave's situation, but my father certainly could. I thank the Lord for godly parents. One other thing that just really blesses me, Jim, was your question to Dave, "Are your parents still praying for you?" It's really a neat thing for me to realize that as I teach my Sunday school class . . .

as I deal with people in counseling and as I pray with kids and neighbors and friends, as I work in the church . . . that my mother is praying hours every day that God's will would be done in our lives and that souls would be won and snatched from the gates of hell. Man! I'm telling you, that is exciting!

There is a quote that says, "Pride is thinking that you have done for yourself what God and other people have done for you." When I think of my mother praying, I just thank God that the things He has done through me are not my doing; the credit is due to that woman who's been out there on her knees praying. I feel so strongly about this issue, and if there's anything that I want to do for my children, it is to bathe them in prayer.

Dr. Dobson, Jr.: Aarlie, do you want to make any closing comment?

Mrs. Hull: I have benefited more than anybody by being here.

Dr. Hernandez: It is so important that this book be not just a compilation of problems and indictments, but a book of hope and optimism for the future of the family. It is facing serious threats and dangers at this time, but God has answers for every question. Bill Gaither's song says, "Because He Lives, I Can Face Tomorrow." That is the source of our hope.

Dr. Dobson, Jr.: You know, Shirley and I ran across a scripture the other day that should inspire everyone who is going through hard times. It offers fantastic hope to those facing some of the difficulties we've been talking about. And when my life begins to fall apart, as I know it eventually will, I'm going to return to this scripture and hold it like a life preserver. It's found in Hab. 3:17-19, and I'm reading from *The*

Living Bible: "Even though the fig trees are all destroyed, and there's neither blossom left nor fruit, and though the olive crops all fail, and the fields lie barren; even if the flocks die in the fields, and the cattle barns are empty, *yet I will rejoice in the Lord;* I will be happy in the God of my salvation. The Lord God is my strength, and he will give me the speed of a deer and bring me safely over the mountain." Isn't that a beautiful promise?

Rev. Dobson, Sr.: We used to sing a song that says, "I feel like traveling on." It misses the point. I've got something that's going to help me make it whether I feel like traveling on or not.

Dr. Dobosn, Jr.: I want to thank each of you for coming to our home and participating in this project. God has been here, too, and I believe He will bless what we've said these past two days.

Appendix

Listed below are examples of family-related topics which should be discussed annually in young adult Sunday school classes. Every item can be supported by biblical references which serve as guiding principles.

A. Christian Parenthood
   1. Biblical principles of disciplining children
   2. Teaching Christian responsibility to children

3. Teaching children about death, life after death, heaven and hell
4. Teaching children the nature of God (the fear of the Lord, the love of God, the mercy of God, etc.)
5. Christian parenthood during the child's adolescence
6. Controlling television in the home
7. Building self-esteem in children
8. Teaching sex education to children

B. Preservation of Marriage
1. Husband and wife roles, as prescribed by the Bible
2. Women's liberation movement and the Christian housewife
3. Christian attitudes toward marital sex
4. Establishing meaningful family devotions
5. The biblical concept of romantic love
6. Christian attitudes toward in-laws and relatives

C. Emotions in the Christian Life
1. The interpretation of guilt
2. The role of impressions in interpreting the will of God
3. Learning to depend on God in time of stress
4. The interpretation of anger
5. Christian perspectives on trouble (Why do Christians have to suffer? Does God always answer the prayer for healing? etc.)
6. The difference between pride, which God despises, and self-esteem, which He endorses
7. Dealing with low self-esteem as a Christian adult

D. Financial Pressures
1. Biblical principles applied to family financial management
2. Tithing and stewardship within the family
3. Christian attitudes toward materialism

E. Related Family Topics
1. Serving Christ in an unchristian business or profession
2. Identification of spiritual gifts
3. Winning your neighbors to Christ
4. Attitudes toward aging and the elderly

173

For Further Reading

Beecher and Beecher. *Parents on the Run*. New York: Grosset and Dunlap, 1967.

Christensen, Larry. *The Christian Family*. Minneapolis: Bethany Fellowship, 1970.

Coopersmith, Stanley. *The Antecedents of Self-esteem*. San Francisco: W. H. Freeman and Co., n.d.

Dobson, James. *Dare to Discipline*. Wheaton, Ill.: Tyndale House Publishers, 1970.

————. *Hide or Seek*. Old Tappan, N.J.: Fleming H. Revell Co., 1974.

————. *What Wives Wish Their Husbands Knew About Women*. Wheaton, Ill.: Tyndale House Publishers, 1975.

Florio, Anthony. *Two to Get Ready*. Old Tappan, N.J.: Fleming H. Revell Co., 1974.

Hendricks, Howard. *Say It with Love*. Wheaton, Ill.: Victor Books, 1972.

————. *Heaven Help the Home!* New York: Berkeley Publishing Corp., 1973.

————. *Families Go Better With Love*. Wheaton, Ill.: Victor Books, 1973.

Jacobsen, Margaret. *The Child in a Christian Home*. Wheaton, Ill.: Scripture Press, 1959.

Jewett, Paul K. *Man as Male and Female*. Grand Rapids, Mich.: Wm. B. Eerdmans Publ. Co., 1974.

LaHaye, Tim. *How to Be Happy Though Married*. Wheaton, Ill.: Tyndale House Publishers, 1968.

————. *How to Win over Depression*. Grand Rapids, Mich.: Zondervan Publishing House, 1974.

————. *Spirit-controlled Temperament*. Wheaton, Ill.: Tyndale House Publishers, 1966.

————. *Transformed Temperaments*. Wheaton, Ill.: Tyndale House Publishers, 1971.

Lee, Mark W. *Our Children: Our Best Friends: Marriage Is a Family Affair*. Grand Rapids, Mich.: Zondervan Publishing House, 1972.

Mace, David R. *The Christian Response to the Sexual Revolution*. Nashville: Abingdon Press, 1970.

Narramore, Bruce. *Help! I'm a Parent*. Grand Rapids, Mich.: Zondervan Publishing House, 1972.

Narramore, Clyde M. *Happiness in Marriage*. Grand Rapids, Mich.: Zondervan Publishing House, 1961.

Patterson and Gullion. *Living with Children*. Champaign, Ill.: Research Press, 1968.

Petersen, J. Allan. *The Marriage Affair*. Wheaton, Ill.: Tyndale House Publishers, 1971.

Richards, Larry. *You the Parent*. Chicago, Ill.: Moody Press, 1974.

——— . *You and Adults*. Chicago, Ill.: Moody Press, 1974.

——— . *You and Youth*. Chicago, Ill.: Moody Press, 1973.

Scanzoni, Letha. *Sex Is a Parent Affair*. Glendale, Calif.: Regal Books, 1973.

Shedd, Charles W. *Letters to Karen: On Keeping Love in Marriage*. Revell and Abingdon, 1965.

——— . *Letters to Philip*. Old Tappan, N.J.: Fleming H. Revell Co., 1968.

——— . *Is Your Family Turned On? Coping with the Drug Culture*. Waco, Tex.: Word Books, 1971.

Small, Dwight Hervey. *Design for Christian Marriage*. Old Tappan, N.J.: Fleming H. Revell Co., 1959.

——— . *After You've Said I Do*. Old Tappan, N.J.: Fleming H. Revell Co., 1968.

——— . *Christian, Celebrate Your Sexuality*. Old Tappan, N.J.: Fleming H. Revell Co., 1974.

Wright, H. Norman. *Communication: Key to Your Marriage*. Glendale, Calif.: Regal Books, 1974.

——— . *The Living Marriage* (Illust.). Old Tappan, N.J.: Fleming H. Revell Co., 1975.

OTHER MATERIALS FOR THE FAMILY
BY DR. JAMES DOBSON

Books:

Dare to Discipline, Tyndale House Publishers, 1970. (Over 500,000 copies of this text have been sold.)

Hide or Seek, Self-esteem for the Child, Fleming Revell Publishing Co., 1974.

The Mentally Retarded Child and his Family, Brunner-Mazel Publishers, 1970. (This book was coedited with Dr. Richard Koch.)

What Wives Wish Their Husbands Knew About Women, Tyndale House Publishers, 1975.

Cassette Tape Recordings:

Dare to Discipline, Vision House Publishers (One Way Library). This album contains six cassette tapes, based on the concepts discussed in the book by the same name.

Preparing for Adolescence, Vision House Publishers (One Way Library). This album contains six cassette tapes, designed to help the pre-teen-ager prepare for the experiences to come.

Self-esteem for the Child, Vision House Publishers (One Way Library). This album contains four cassette tapes and presents the ways parents and teachers can maximize self-confidence in children.

These items are available in local bookstores or can be ordered by writing Box 952, Temple City, Calif. 91780. Dr. Dobson can also be contacted through that address, although he regrets that he is unable to respond to requests for personal consultation.